Bridge My Way

Zia Mahmood

Bridge Consultant and Editor
Phillip Alder

Natco Press

Natco Press
181 Longhill Rd. I-6
Little Falls, NJ 07424
201-890-9375
Fax: 201-890-0602

Printed in the United States of America
ISBN 0-9634715-2-X

Contents

Acknowledgments

First, to the St James Club, Antigua, Michelle, Vivenne and the crab for my most enjoyable stay.

Second, to Nael Islam for help in typing the manuscript. What a way to spend a honeymoon!

To Micki Beenu and Rosita because they'll kill me if I don't mention them.

To Masood Salim, my good friend and partner for 20 years.

To David Burn for his help, especially at the original galley-proof stage.

To Estee Griffin, for her American editing.

To Phillip Alder, without whose help this book would never have been written, in this century at least. He gave invaluable assistance in researching material, editing my prose, and in preparing the original manuscript.

To my American publishers, Pamela and Matthew Granovetter, for their friendship over the years.

But most of all . . .

To my mother

Bridge My Way

Zia Mahmood

1

Falling in Love

One million pounds . . . that's the largest bet I've ever made. You might think that makes me a big-time gambler. Not at all — just a bridge player.

You see, I wasn't taking a crazy risk when I made the bet, which was that no one could write a computer program to beat me at the game of bridge. I was betting on a sure thing.

The world has an idea that bridge is a mathematical game, and that you need a computer-type mind to enjoy it and play it well. The world is wrong. The people who actually play bridge know better, and that is why this challenge, made on national TV in England, apparently so full of bravado, was never taken up. It did, however, attract a few interesting letters to the BBC, like the following:

> Dear Sir:
> For some time I have been following Mr. Mahmood around the Tournament Circuit without him knowing it. I am almost ready

to take up the bet, but need a small amount of assistance to finish my research. Would an advance of £20,000 be possible? Can you help?

Thank you.

Another:

Dear Sir:

I could easily arrange to invent a computer program to beat Mr. Mahmood and win the million pounds. However, I am slightly inconvenienced at the moment, as I am serving a 15-year jail sentence. If you could arrange an early parole, I am sure I would be happy to take up and win the bet.

The Weasel burst in, interrupting my story.

"Zia you must have been nuts; you were absolutely crazy! Everybody knows that computers can't play bridge. Even my daughter could have won that bet, and she's only nine years old."

Paul Trent, known affectionately as the Weasel, is a tough, professional bridge player from New York, who plays for high stakes. I'm not sure how he got the name, but I've a suspicion it's partly because he plays the cards with incredible speed, dexterously slipping in and out of dangerous contracts. Also, with his small frame and sharp features, he looks a lot like a weasel.

It was early afternoon, Sunday, May 6, 1990, and the Weasel was one of three people in a car that was speeding away from the muggers and madness of New York. We were heading to the normally avoidable, but for once very inviting, gambling town of Atlantic City.

I say avoidable because to anyone who has experienced the style of the more elegant casinos of Europe, Atlantic City is a horror. The better-known Las Vegas has some atmosphere; Atlantic City has none.

Forget the James Bond image of beautiful people dressed in perfectly cut evening clothes sipping champagne. Think instead of fat, sweaty people with buckets full of coins and a uniform of T-shirt, shorts and sneakers.

Forget the thought of emotionless elegance while a player coolly wins a fortune at the baccarat table. Picture instead a yelp and an "All right, you sucker!" as a taxi-driver from New Jersey wins seven dollars in quarters from a one-armed bandit and celebrates with a hot-dog.

To be fair, Las Vegas has some great shows, cabarets performed by really excellent entertainers. Even Atlantic City has the occasional superstar, but the quality sinks rapidly in anything except these shows.

"Not so crazy. If you're going to make a bet that large, there's no harm in having the odds stacked in your favor."

This came from Tim "Mr. Backgammon" Holland. Well dressed and well traveled, Tim is a talented guy: an expert's expert at backgammon, golf and bridge. And he knows about making bets; he has been making them for most of his life. Considering his large number of ex-wives and his even larger alimony payments, I have a feeling those bets have been more than slightly successful.

We were headed to the S— Hotel, where on Monday we would sit down at the tables and take part in the most lucrative bridge tournament ever held: the Omar Sharif Individual World Championship. From a total purse of $200,000, the first prize was a juicy $40,000.

More than 200 bridge players from all over the world would be coming to the city. Most of them would be sharp-witted and skillful; all of them would be hungry for victory.

It reminded me a bit of an old Western, where all the best gunslingers were riding into town for a shoot-out to find out who was the fastest.

"How do we rate your chances, Zia?" Tim continued. "You know you must be one of the favorites."

I was about to protest indignantly that in an event like this it was impossible to have a favorite. There were too many good players, too many imponderables. No one would play with his regular partner; you would play with someone different every round, someone you probably had never even played with before. It would be a lottery.

But I reverted to type when I answered, "I feel good, Tim. I'm going to win."

If you're going to fight a war, you'd better not think about losing. And returning to my earlier gunslinger analogy, I *was* the fastest, I *was* the best, and when the dust had settled in four days' time, I had every intention of being the last one standing, guns smoking victorious. I wanted to win, not just for the money, although this was certainly attractive, but because the winner would earn the undisputed right to be called the best individual bridge player in the world.

I deserved that right.

Do you remember Edward G. Robinson in *The Cincinnati Kid?* Well, today I was The Man. It was *my* game. It had taken me a long time to earn this position, but today it was mine, and no fresh kid was going to get lucky and take it away from me.

A long time, I thought. It had been almost 20 years. Looking back, it seems strange to think about the years when I didn't play bridge. How *does* someone become a full-time bridge player? Become that rare animal, something between an artist and a hustler, who wanders the world like a nomad, looking for the next game, searching constantly yet forlornly for the elusive perfect hand.

Early Years

I was born in Pakistan, into one of the powerful "Twenty Families," as they are called. The men were traditionally expected to become businessmen or politicians, and the children had marriages arranged by their parents, a system that somehow worked then and still works remarkably successfully today.

My father died in a plane crash when I was very young. One of the few things found in the wreckage was his briefcase. Inside was a sheet of paper detailing all his assets. It seems that when he realized that the plane was going to crash, he wrote them all down on paper, then carefully locked the sheets in his briefcase.

My mother was a remarkable woman, who was a rebel by the standards of the day. In a strongly Muslim country where women usually stay at home and raise families, she became a gynecologist — at that time, a move almost unheard of for a woman. She would administer to the wealthy and the poor alike. The only difference was that she charged the wealthy, using those fees to subsidize her treatment of the poor.

When my father died, my mother decided that she would move to England to further her career. Another good reason for this move was to give my brother and me an English education, much favored at the time in Pakistan. We were sent to the very British Rugby Public School.

I did well and enjoyed sports but hated the traditions and rules. I couldn't see the logic in not being permitted to carry an umbrella in the rain, or why healthy young boys weren't allowed to mix with healthy young girls. I studied foreign languages, not the higher mathematics that, according to popular misconception, bridge players need.

However, I suppose I must admit that I enjoyed the experience as a whole, and I can thank the school for two tangible advantages that have affected my life.

First, several years after I left school my brother was sent to jail in Pakistan for being in the opposition political party. Unlike the British, our system was not such that you could stand on a soapbox at Hyde Park Corner and criticize the government; if you tried to air your views, the soapbox was likely to be shot at — and you along with it.

My brother was kept in prison for a year, part of the time in solitary confinement — a frightening ordeal. Regularly, he heard fellow prisoners being beaten, and he had scorpions (without their stings, though he didn't know it at the time) thrown into his cell.

Altogether a rather harrowing experience, you might think. Apparently not. When the case was finally thrown out by the Supreme Court for having been fabricated, my brother's first comment upon being released from jail was, "Thank God for Rugby. After that, jail was almost comfortable!"

Second, in our final term, the graduates were addressed by the Headmaster. He gave us a talk about the outside world and life. For most of us, this was too late, because we were already well down the road to ruin. But he did say one thing that has stuck in my mind. "Some time in your life you'll come to a moment when you will ask yourself the question, 'Should I get married to so-and-so?' When that times comes, my advice is *don't* get married. But if ever a day comes when you think to yourself, 'I *must* get married to so-and-so, I can't wait,' that's the time. You've found the right person."

I'm not sure whether I should blame him or thank him, but the advice still sounds good. I was a bachelor then and I happily remain one today.

At seventeen I had the choice of staying on at Rugby, with the intention of trying for a place at Oxford, or leaving immediately for the temptation and flesh-pots of London. I chose London.

I eventually decided to become a chartered accountant. I was to find that it is the only profeession with a more boring image than bridge.

Even so, I joined an accounting firm in the City, and launched myself into the London of the Swinging Sixties. Carnaby Street was full of color; new dance crazes appeared almost daily; the Beatles and Rolling Stones were idolized; the night-clubs were buzzing.

Almost overnight clothes were metamorphosed from stark to sexy. I remember struggling bleary-eyed into work one morning and seeing my friend and fellow trainee David smiling all over his face. David was a great guy, but happened to be Jewish, Indian and a dwarf! Luckily, he had a terrific sense of humor. I was in a foul mood, having lost in a casino the night before. "David," I said, "you're Jewish, Indian and a dwarf — what have you got to be so happy about?"

His grin grew even wider as he answered. "Somebody called Mary Quant just invented the mini-skirt. How would you feel if you were as short as me?"

This was the age of free love, flower power and long hair. It was impossible not to be caught up in the atmosphere. I wasn't exactly a hippie, but nobody would have said I was the conventional city type either. With due respect to the British city image, it was and is far removed from my style. This sometimes caused me problems. I remember a partner at my very conservative accounting firm telling me to get my hair cut. Naturally, I arrived late for work the next morning, having been to the barber.

"Why did you have your hair cut in office time?"

"It grows in office time."

"It doesn't all grow in office time."

"I didn't have it all cut off."

That was either nimble repartee or too much *chutzpah*, depending on where you come from.

I suppose it wasn't surprising that I was soon fired from this particular firm. I found ticking ledgers and other routine work exceedingly boring, and spent as much time as possible enjoying life. For me, this meant playing cards and pursuing women. Not long after, though, I joined a much smaller, less traditional accounting form. There was an existing staff of three, I made it four. The one and only partner was the treasurer of Hendon Dog Track. He was a man after my own heart, and I found working there much more my style.

The distractions were not good for my career advancement, and I failed the exams comfortably the first time. But I wasn't worried; in the '60s it was easy to be happy. I was having a great time, and bridge was the furthest thing from my mind. Cards, on the other hand, I did find interesting — though I played only poker and blackjack. For a time I even moonlighted as a croupier in a poker club. There I met some of the more interesting — and more dangerous — members of the London club world. One of them was Lucky Gordon, of Christine Keeler fame, who sang songs like Nat King Cole while taking my money at rummy like Al Capone.

Another, a neanderthal called Man Mountain, lost heavily one evening. Being of a rather primitive mind, he took out his frustrations by almost destroying the club and the people in it, including me. I found that a convincing argument for staying away from the world of gambling. It was some time before I returned to the tables, concentrating instead on my studies.

After somehow managing to pass the exams the second time around, I found myself a qualified accountant. I was 22 years old. Almost immediately afterward my mother died suddenly. So I returned home to Pakistan where, for a while, I did what I was trained to do — work. I ran the family newspaper business.

Falling in Love

In marked contrast to London in the '60s, the social scene for the young in Pakistan was limited, girls traditionally being kept at home until marriage. At the time, I was trying to get better acquainted with an attractive young woman whom I knew only slightly. The good news was that she finally agreed to meet me. The bad news was that the venue was a bridge party. It wasn't my idea of a perfect date (as I couldn't even play bridge), but it was better than nothing. I had, of course, told my date that I could play. To avoid looking too foolish, I picked up a book, Alfred Sheinwold's *Five Weeks to Winning Bridge*. I hoped that I could compress those five weeks into just three days. Much to my surprise, I found the book interesting.

The big day arrived and, as you can imagine, I performed embarrassingly badly — though I just about managed to save myself from complete exposure. But I was sufficiently intrigued by the game that my concentration was diverted from the girl — my reason for being there in the first place — to the intricacies of the game.

That was almost the last I saw of her. I became enthralled; the spark had been lit, and soon became a fire. No, not a fire, more like a furnace. Over the next few months I read all the bridge books I could lay my hands on. My intention was to learn the rules and techniques, but through their pages, I was also introduced to the fascinating people who inhabited the world of bridge. People like the showman Ely Culbertson, who had promoted the game by his eccentric behavior, extravagant boasts and famous challenge matches. He had been to bridge what Muhammad Ali was to boxing.

I read of the remarkable feats of the invincible Italian Blue Team, the *Squaddra Azzurra*. Its heroes, Benito Garozzo, Giorgio Belladonna and Pietro Forquet, had monopolized world bridge for years, and I marvelled at the genius of their play.

I learned how Ira Corn, a Texas millionaire and bridge fanatic, resolved to bring the world championship back to America. He hired a team of the best professionals, housed them in Dallas, gave them a coach (a retired army man), and made them train full time, like soldiers, to be physically and mentally prepared to win. His strategy worked — the team, the Aces, won the Bermuda Bowl in 1971.

At that time, it never occurred to me that many of these people would become my friends, some even my partners.

Two books stuck vividly in my mind. *Right Through the Pack*, by Robert Darvas and Norman de Villiers Hart, a charming fairy-tale collection of bridge hands; and Terence Reese's *Play Bridge with Reese*. I have read both of them many times and recommend them unreservedly.

Hooked, I started to play daily with a group of friends. Like all beginners, I experienced mostly frustration. I would finally master one point only to find that there were many others to learn and conquer. But I remember the pleasure, the mixture of pride and satisfaction, after making a good play — a feeling no non-bridge player can understand.

When I take an interest in something, I become a fanatic. I can't help it; I become totally obsessed. I was determined not just to learn the game but to master it and become an expert player. I was in a hurry, too, which didn't help. But learning was such fun that the time flew by painlessly, and I started to get better.

Non-bridge players, scared to take up the game, always protest, "I'm sure you must be very good at numbers!" or, "You must have started when you were very young." Neither could be further from the truth. You might need to be able to count to 13 — which most people have been able to do since they were two or three years old. The only tough calculation I ever have to make is after the game, when I add up how much money I've won or lost on the day. So much for arithmetic.

I started to learn the game at the age of 24. I had never even thought about bridge before that. If you have a talent or just an interest, age isn't that important. Having mentioned talent, it is interesting to speculate about just what qualities or talents are required by a bridge player. Which type of person does well at the game?

These are tough questions to answer. To try to uncover the truth, I asked 50 of the world's best players to give me one word to describe a top bridge player. What did I find out? Nothing! Or, more accurately, the answers varied so much that it appears nobody has any real idea. Here are some of the words they came up with: imagination, intensity, concentration, talent, judgment, stamina, logic, focus, awareness, card-sense, desire to win, technique, determination, creativity, quickness of thought, discipline, dedication, consistency, psychology, temperament, confidence. In other words, anything and everything. I don't think there is anyone who wouldn't identify with at least one of these words, probably with several. Still, it is interesting to note that not one person mentioned mathematics in any shape or form.

The truth is that the best players have greatly varied personalities and characteristics. All sorts of people can succeed in bridge; there is no stereotype for the perfect player, and every player will emphasize the importance of different qualities. For my part, I think the three most important talents are a logical and clear-thinking mind, card-sense, and a positive mental attitude. Ideally, a mixture of Solomon, Nick the Greek and Muhammad Ali.

There is one more thing, a trait rather than a talent. I have found that most top players have enormous egos. I am no exception in this respect, indeed, am sometimes cited as one of the worst offenders! My excuse, if I need one, is that it's necessary to remain strong and confident in one's own ability. It is easier to win when you are the best — or when at least you think you are.

Someone once asked the American player Bob Hamman, one of the greatest players of all time and a good friend, if he thought anybody else played as well as he does. He thought it over for a moment and then replied, "Maybe God — on a good day!" I think he was just being modest. . . .

After about six months of fanatical playing and reading, of

regularly falling asleep at work, and of being ostracized and abused by non-bridge-playing friends, things were getting better. I can still recall the afternoon when I played a hand that reduced to this three-card ending:

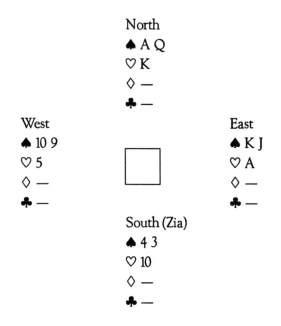

North
♠ A Q
♡ K
◊ —
♣ —

West
♠ 10 9
♡ 5
◊ —
♣ —

East
♠ K J
♡ A
◊ —
♣ —

South (Zia)
♠ 4 3
♡ 10
◊ —
♣ —

As South, needing to win two out of the three tricks to make the contract, I was just about to take the spade finesse when somewhere a light dawned. Instead I led the ♡10, endplaying East to lead from the ♠K-J. Looking back now, it's no big deal, but at the time I was euphoric. I relived the play in my mind time and again and couldn't wait for another chance to execute an endplay. I suppose that was the point of no return. From that moment the game had me — I was addicted.

It was here that fate intervened. It was 1975 and the Oil Boom in the Middle East had just begun. The feeling in the oil-rich countries was like during the Klondike Gold Rush — with fortunes waiting to be made. My brother, always the businessman, was disillusioned by Pakistan and his period in jail. He thought it was a good time for us to try our luck elsewhere. So we moved to Abu Dhabi, previously a desert oasis in the Arab Emirates, but then a wealthy country expanding rapidly.

My brother was right. At the end of one year, our business looked as though it would succeed. Despite this, I was reluctant to stay in Abu Dhabi; a year is a long time if it is full of hard work. I was allergic to the regimen, the heat and, most important of all, the lack of bridge.

I had visited bridge clubs on my occasional trips to London, and, though I played for modest stakes, I found that I won far more often than I lost. I itched to get on with playing and learning the game full time.

When I discussed these thoughts with my family and friends their reaction ranged from disapproval to horror. I received comments like, "People don't play bridge full time." "It's just a game; you might as well try tiddleywinks." "Stick with the business."

They say the world is full of willing people — those willing to work, and those willing to let them. I am firmly in the second category.

Being a life-long member of the Black Sheep of the Family Club, if I'm advised to do something, invariably I do the opposite. I decided to roll the dice, and caught the next plane to London. I left my share of the business in my brother's more-than-capable hands, telling him to invest it as he saw fit. I took £1,000 with me, £500 for rent and £500 for a stake at the bridge club.

I still remember my brother's parting words: "If you are going to spend the rest of your life playing a game, then at least become the best."

23

2

Better a Live Chicken
Than a Dead Duck

Atlantic City, the Cocktail Party

Sunday, May 6, 1990. The S— Hotel was exactly what I expected a casino hotel to be: gaudy, glitzy, noisy and thoroughly uninviting. But that didn't matter, because a bridge tournament can transform any atmosphere. As I walked in, I could almost smell the anticipation and excitement.

At the check-in counters there were long lines of familiar faces, and everyone was in a hurry. We barely had time to check in and change before the start of the cocktail party that Omar Sharif was hosting for the players. By the time I came downstairs, the party was buzzing. The room was full of bridge players and casino promotion people, the latter smiling effusively and greeting everyone. By financing the tournament, the casino owners were, of course, hoping to make money. They expected that in the evening, after the bridge sessions, the players would frequent the tables and lose enough to make the investment worthwhile.

For those of you who are not familiar with gambling, there is no game played in the casino where the player has the odds in his favor — except, at times, blackjack. There, a good player, who counts the cards (it is not as difficult as it sounds, although the casino staff will hassle you if they realize you are counting) and follows the odds, can win over a period. To win at blackjack, read *Beat the Dealer* by Edward Thorpe. The author is a professor at the University of California who used a computer to help develop a system for beating the casino at blackjack. He arranged financial backing and proved his method at the tables in Las Vegas. As a result, casinos changed their rules, but the method still works.

Two very popular games in the casino are craps and roulette. Craps allows two of the least unfavorable bets for the unknowledgeable gambler, while roulette is a quick and enjoyable road to bankruptcy.

The unwritten law in all casinos is: Make sure the "punter" has no chance in the long run. That's the way it's set up, and it's very successful. If you think you can beat a casino, forget it. There is no system, there is no formula. Gamble all you like, but only if you are prepared to lose. That way you won't be surprised or disappointed, because, believe me, you will lose in the long run.

There was a strong international flavor to the gathering. The majority, of course, were American, but there were players from all parts of the globe: Britain, Sweden, Israel, India, Poland,* even Russia. However, there was only one Pakistani. I was heavily outnumbered, but on reflection I decided that one was all it took to win a tournament.

---

*Bridge is very popular in Poland, and Poles are among the best international players. Their popularity is high among other players because they come armed with large supplies of caviar and vodka, which they sell to the participants. The dollar works overtime in Poland and the proceeds from sales at bridge tournaments help them to get through the harsh winters in Warsaw.

I was looking around for a waiter when I heard someone shouting, "Zia, I've got a proposition for you."

I recognized the voice and immediately started to slink away, but before I could move more than a couple of paces, "Mike" was at my side, pinning me down. Mike is a real New Yorker, quick-witted, brash, and a street fighter. Amusing at times, he knows all the angles and usually manages to end up on the winning side of a bet. Like all survivors, he is a born salesman who could sell a third-hand bicycle to a second-hand car dealer.

His propositions are to be avoided at all costs. I know of at least half-a-dozen people who have accepted the following "offer": "I will give you $100 cash now if you promise to give me all the coins in your pocket whenever I see you." They soon regretted their folly.

He continued, "I bet you can't give me the correct answer to this little problem." I was already sure he was right. If someone, anyone, ever comes up to you and starts with this sentence, believe them and don't bet against them — you'll end up a loser.

In *Guys and Dolls*, when Nathan Detroit makes him a proposition, the gambler, Sky Masterson, replies, "When I left home my daddy told me, 'One day a man will come up to you and show you a brand new deck of cards, and bet you that the jack of spades will jump out and pour cider in your ear. When that day comes, don't take the bet because you *will* end up with an ear full of cider." Never take a sucker bet. This sounded like one.

"Mike," I said, "I have to see someone. I'll talk to you later."

It was too late; he had me by the arm. "Let's make a small bet," he insisted. "How about loser commits suicide?"

Typical — only he could think up a bet like that. I almost suggested that the loser murder the other person, but instead said that I would bet one dinner at a restaurant of the winner's choice back in New York.

Happy to have captured his "audience," Mike relaxed. "You're a contestant on a quiz show, a kind of *Let's Make a Deal*. You are shown three doors and told there is a Rolls Royce behind one of them and booby prizes behind the others. You choose one. Now the quizmaster, who knows where the Rolls is, must open one of the remaining two doors, one behind which he knows there is a booby prize. Then he offers you the chance to stay with the door you chose or to change to the other unopened door. What should you do?

"Should you stick with your choice, change, or is it a 50-50 guess? Well, what do you think?"

I considered for a moment, almost preferring to lose a dinner and get away than spend ages contemplating the problem. But I hate losing, so I gave it some thought. It seemed to be a 50-50 proposition. I was about to say that when I paused. One thing was for sure — Mike is a devious guy and would never have brought this up if the answer was so obvious. Deciding that betting on the psychology of the individual was better than nothing, I took a chance. "I change doors," I said.

I could tell by his hurt expression that I had got lucky. But it was only a moment before Mike was back on the offensive. "You're right; I owe you a dinner. But how did you work it out? Do you know why?"

I didn't have the slightest clue but had no intention of admitting it. I did know enough to quit while I was ahead. I smiled knowingly and made a dash for it.

Later, I thought about it carefully and did work out the answer. Here's the reasoning: Let's call the doors A, B and C. In each case we choose A. There are three possibilities:

1. The Rolls Royce is indeed behind A. After we choose A, the quizmaster opens B (or it could have been C, which also has a booby prize behind the door) and offers us C. We accept and change our choice. We lose the Rolls Royce.

2. The Rolls Royce is behind B. The quizmaster opens C

(he is not allowed to open B this time because the Rolls Royce is there) and offers us B. We accept and win the Rolls Royce.

3. The Rolls Royce is behind C. The quizmaster opens B (he is not allowed to open C) and offers us C. We accept, changing our choice from A to C. We win the Rolls Royce.

As you can see, the odds are actually 2-to-1 to change doors. It didn't look like it at first; it is a kind of optical illusion. The argument is like the Principle of Restricted Choice in bridge. Consider this situation:

Dummy

♠ A J 10 6

□

Declarer (You)

♠ 8 7 5 4 2

You can afford only one spade loser, but both the king and queen are out. You lead low from hand and finesse the ♠10. East wins with, say, the king. When you regain the lead in hand, you lead a second low spade — with the queen still out — do you finesse the jack or play the ace?

The Principle of Restricted Choice states that when an opponent plays a specific card from two that he might have played, it implies he had no choice. Just as when the quizmaster chooses one particular door, it suggests that he had no choice — the other door was not available to him. Here, East had to win with the king earlier because he didn't have the queen. On the second round, you should therefore finesse the jack, not put up the ace.

I managed to find Omar and some friends, and we went to dinner, compliments of the casino. Naturally Omar had to sign autographs and have his photo taken with various waitresses. As usual, he took it all in stride, smiling and agreeing patiently to the requests.

As expected, the food turned out to be pretty bad, but the wine was first class. The conversation was mostly about bridge, with one of the Americans arguing with Paul Chemla as to the relative merits of French and American bidding methods. Nobody won the argument, but Chemla took on all the Americans at the table and outshouted them all. The subject finally subsided as we rose to leave the table.

* * * * * * * * *

London, 1975

I felt a shiver of fear as Godzilla beckoned me with his long hairy arm. Simultaneously two words rang out across the room: "Table up!"

"Come and make up the table, Zia," he growled.

There are more than two million bridge players in Britain, and most of them recognize the familiar cry heard in bridge clubs to signify the end of a rubber. I was in London, at Stefan's Bridge Club (now vanished), perched above a Wimpy Bar in the Edgeware Road. I was eager for my turn to cut in at a 50p table, where I regularly killed my none-too-skillful opponents. There were the usual half-dozen games in progress. The stakes varied from a mere 10 pence a point to a not so mere £100 a point. (In London, a point means the 100 points needed for game; unlike in America, where a point is a point. In America 10 pence a point would be equivalent to 10 pounds a point in Britain.) At £100 a point, a rubber can easily cost someone over £1,000. I was still getting better, with my sights set on moving up in stakes as my game improved.

The club was not the most elegant of places — bridge clubs rarely are — but it had its own atmosphere. Like all bridge clubs, its clientele was a real mixture, ranging from businessmen and other professional people, who dropped in for a quick game after work, down to night players and the elite of the gambling underworld. Sprinkled in between were a few housewives, insomniacs and the odd "professional."

There were our regulars. Then there was Godzilla.

Have you ever approached a bridge table praying that you don't cut one of the players?

Godzilla is that person — and more.

Have you ever seen a game in progress and decided not to cut in because of an unpleasant player still in?

Godzilla is that person — and more.

After the most dreadful results, have you ever wanted to take your partner's throat in your hands and squeeze until his eyes bulged?

I'm beginning to think you must know Godzilla. He is an ape of such proportions that he makes King Kong look like an apology for a primate. He is worse than "your worst nightmare" — he is *real*.

Away from the bridge table, Godzilla is an amiable, well-mannered, even cultured, man, originally of East European extraction. If you sat at the dinner table with him, you could be confident he would select the perfect wines to complement the food, and that his conversation would be lively and entertaining. But sit down at the bridge table and something happens — *snap*, he transforms into Godzilla, the most dangerous monster. He makes a holiday at Transylvania with Count Dracula seem inviting.

His bidding is bestial. He uses the Unusual Notrump — normally used to show at least 5-5 in the minors — with four-card suits. He doubles the opponents in a game when they were about to bid a hopeless slam. He doesn't stop bidding a five-card suit until the opponents stamp on him and chop him into little pieces. His atrocities are legendary and almost beyond belief. Which was his most horrible hand? No one knows for sure, but the consensus is that the following is a strong candidate:

South dealer
All vulnerable

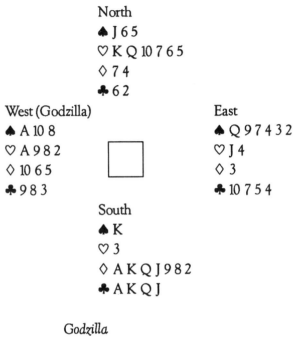

North
♠ J 6 5
♡ K Q 10 7 6 5
◇ 7 4
♣ 6 2

West (Godzilla)
♠ A 10 8
♡ A 9 8 2
◇ 10 6 5
♣ 9 8 3

East
♠ Q 9 7 4 3 2
♡ J 4
◇ 3
♣ 10 7 5 4

South
♠ K
♡ 3
◇ A K Q J 9 8 2
♣ A K Q J

	Godzilla		
South	West	North	East
2 ♣*	pass	2 ◇*	pass
4 NT	pass	5 ♡	pass
7 NT	double	(all pass)	

2 ♣ = strong, artificial and forcing
2 ◇ = negative response; fewer than nine points.

South meant four notrump as Blackwood, but North thought — correctly, because there is no suit agreement — it was natural, showing a balanced hand of 28-30 points, and bid his heart suit. South, taking this as indicating two aces, bid a rapid seven notrump!

Godzilla finally saw a contract he knew he could beat, and doubled. Godzilla is well read. Nearly every authority tells

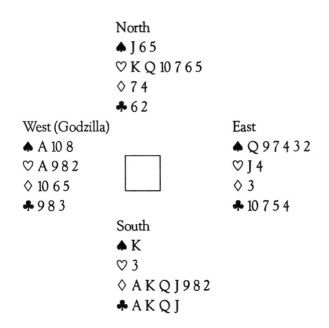

North
♠ J 6 5
♡ K Q 10 7 6 5
♦ 7 4
♣ 6 2

West (Godzilla)
♠ A 10 8
♡ A 9 8 2
♦ 10 6 5
♣ 9 8 3

East
♠ Q 9 7 4 3 2
♡ J 4
♦ 3
♣ 10 7 5 4

South
♠ K
♡ 3
♦ A K Q J 9 8 2
♣ A K Q J

you to lead fourth-highest from your longest and strongest.
So he followed instructions. He led . . . the *two* of hearts!

South played dummy's king, and then ran all his minor-
suit winners. At trick 12, Godzilla had to choose between
discarding his ♠A and his ♡A. He looked around vainly for
inspiration. He looked for the answer on the ceiling, he
searched for it on all the walls, even on the carpet under the
table. But finally he guessed wrongly and threw away the ♠A
— seven notrump doubled and made! No wonder I tremble
at his call.

* * * * * * * * *

Sunday Evening

Back in Atlantic City, the gamblers prepared to attack the
casino tables.

Do you have the impression that bridge players in a
tournament go to bed at 9 p.m. to rest properly before the
mental exertions of the morrow? Nothing like it. Most bridge
players are insomniacs who wake up with a hangover half an

hour before game time, which is usually 1 p.m. in America. Walking into the gaming room, the first thing I noticed was that it was packed with bridge players, who were mostly divided between the blackjack and the craps tables. Omar and Chemla gravitated to the craps table, while I decided to check out the blackjack games and looked for the "right" table. I'm not usually big on superstitions, but there is no point in fighting Lady Luck. If there is a table where the croupier has been very lucky, systematically beating all the players, it is sensible to try somewhere else.

I soon saw a table where I belonged for at least three reasons. First, a good friend of mine, Alan Sontag, author of *The Bridge Bum*, was already playing there. Sonty has a computer for a brain, and is a card-counting blackjack player. I could let him do the hard work of counting the cards, making smaller or bigger bets in synch with him. There were no guarantees of winning but I felt I'd at least be getting the best value for my money.

Second, the croupier — Sarah Jane according to her name tag — was a blond with a stunning smile; she was almost pretty enough to make me think I wouldn't mind losing.

Third, the table was occupied completely with "bridgies," who seemed to be enjoying themselves. This meant that they had to be winning. I changed some cash into chips and settled into the game.

The players were knowledgeable, hitting on 16 when the dealer had a 7, 8 or 9; and doubling down correctly on 9, 10 or 11 when the dealer had a low card. Things started well, and, for a time I joined everyone in winning. The mentality of a blackjack player is such that he has warm feelings for the croupier as long as he wins. But this changes immediately if he starts losing. This is despite knowing the croupier has no control over the cards being dealt. Casinos don't need to cheat; they win too much to risk it.

Sarah Jane, our croupier, turned out to be friendly, with a

sense of humor. While I was winning I promised to send her a present of two racing camels if she kept up the flow of good cards. Not surprising, she turned down the camels, but laughingly invited me to make a better offer. I was just about to include a few sheep and an oil-well when the luck started to change. Things went downhill rapidly, so I refrained from making the offer I was sure she couldn't refuse.

Soon, some of the other players gave vent to their frustration. Sarah Jane was sympathetic, well used to this reaction. She kept smiling but kept also her incredible run of luck. She wiped out all our winnings and then some. I took this as a hint that she didn't like camels or sheep, let alone Pakistani bridge players, and I got out of there before she killed me. Round one to Sarah Jane.

Loafing around, I passed by a roulette table. Betting on roulette is very unprofessional, but because no one was watching, I slipped a $10 bet on number 1, secretly thinking that if it came up, it would be a sign that I would win the bridge tournament. Instead, I saw the ball drop sickeningly into 31. Typical.

It was time to move on once again. Omar's craps table was overflowing with players and spectators. Omar himself was rolling the dice and at the same time delighting the audience with jokes and stories. Of course, nearly everybody bet with him, so each winning roll was met by a simultaneous roar that shook the casino and attracted even more watchers. His bets were very large, the only problem being that he kept buying champagne for the watching ladies when he won, while the croupiers greedily swallowed up his bets when he lost — leaving him not much margin for a big win.

Omar made me think of his role as the debonair gambler Nick Arnstein in Funny Girl, and I reflected that he probably didn't have to learn any lines. He was a natural. I considered joining the action, but the crowd was too dense. I decided to call it a day instead.

3

Playing the Table

London, the 1970s

Do you want to start winning immediately? You can!

If I had to give only one lesson to a bridge player — one tip more valuable than any other — it would be an easy task. I wouldn't suggest he learn any advanced techniques such as Keycard Blackwood, Revolving Discards or the Canary Club — the key point is to p*lay the table*. Forget the difficulties entailed in acquiring the techniques of a great bridge player — *just concentrate on being practical.*

Perhaps at the highest echelon the game does boil down to hair-splitting decisions and expert evaluation. But most people are not at this level. Being practical starts with being aware that each of us is different and your characteristics affect your bridge. The next time you sit at a table, look around and consciously put labels on the players. Is this one strong or weak? A gambler? A mouse? A bully? A coward? Logical? Muddled? If you can do that (it isn't so difficult), adapt your game to their traits, using their strengths and weaknesses for your benefit, you're almost there.

"Practical" means understanding that your results are often far more likely to be affected by what your partner had for dinner or whether he had a fight with his wife than by the level of his card-play. S. J. Simon's advice half a century ago is still valid today: You should try for the best possible result, not the best result possible.

Forget intra-finesses — think indigestion! If he looks as if he has had his hands on an extra glass of port with dinner, you'd be well advised to take control and keep his hands off the dummy now. That is where the "money" is made and lost. There is the key.

If you want to be a winner at rubber bridge, remember this lesson: The bottom line is ending up ahead. Forget about the dreamer who said, "Winning is not as important as taking part." I'd like him to meet my bank manager and try offering that as an excuse for the overdraft. More to the point is the statement: "Show me a good loser and I will show you a loser." Don't let yourself have to show the world what a great loser you are.

However, playing the table isn't as simple as it seems. It is probable that the standard of the players in your game varies enormously. It certainly does in my games. Subconsciously decide in your own mind who is the best player by simply looking forward to cutting him. Similarly, pinpoint the worst player by your silent prayer to avoid him. The next step is to use the information to work for you.

There are two parts to this: the handling of your partner and the handling of your opponents. Every time you partner someone, even for one rubber, you cease being an individual and become a unit, like a married couple; the winning strategy is to start thinking like one.

You've heard the saying that a chain is only as strong as its weakest link. That saying could have been invented by a bridge player, because a successful partnership is only as strong as the weaker partner. Partners must be on the same wavelength, and it is pointless speaking to someone in a language he can't understand.

Suppose you picked up this hand:

♠ A 5 4 3   ♡ K 6 5 4   ◇ A Q J 2   ♣ 2

Your partner opens one spade. What would you respond?

No problem, you say, and soon offer your answer. Maybe this is not a problem to you, but for me this question is vital, and not easy at all. In fact, before answering I need to ask a question of my own: "Who are the other players at the table?"

If you can understand the last sentence, believe it and practice it, you are on your way to becoming a bridge player. You see, almost all the time there is *no correct bid or play in bridge*. The correct action depends upon the prevalent conditions and especially on your partner and your opponents. Remember that there is no such thing as an individual action at the table; everything is in the interaction. It is vital to understand this point.

Going back to the hand I just gave you, I could find at least three answers, each eminently correct in different partnerships. If I were partnered with Benito Garozzo, the famous Italian world champion, who loves conventional bids and systems, I would bid four clubs, a splinter bid describing a good hand, trump support and a singleton (or void) in clubs. This bid is descriptive and informative, I know that he'd love the bid and, even more important, he'd understand it.

But if I were playing with Rixi Markus, the great British Women's World Champion, I would respond with a natural two diamonds. Rixi frowns on too much system; her forte is natural bidding. I would describe my hand more slowly, but equally accurately. She would be most upset if I bid four clubs.

Finally, if I held the hand:

$$\spadesuit \, A\,5\,4\,3 \quad \heartsuit \, K\,6\,5\,4 \quad \diamondsuit \, A\,Q\,J\,2 \quad \clubsuit \, 2$$

playing with the weakest player in the club, the dreaded Godzilla, I would bid a direct four spades. It would be pointless and foolish to make a bid such as four clubs or two diamonds, which would confuse him (he might pass the former!) and give information to the opponents. Even if he did realize what I was doing, he might propel us to a slam that he would be bound to misplay. I prefer to score the sure game bonus and give up on a possible slam. The only winning method when playing with a monster is to avoid monstrous losses.

In this case, by bidding four spades, which is the winning bid for the partnership as opposed to the best bid (four clubs or two diamonds), I try to take a plus score. Godzilla may be a weak player, but that's no reason to punish him by giving him a problem he can't solve or a bid he can't understand. Punishing your partner means punishing yourself. I hope you can see the logic of this argument. A winning player is one who understands the different types of players he is seated with, and then uses their strengths and weaknesses to work for him.

It is like an army general employing his forces. Sun Tzu wrote in his book, *The Art of War*, about the Chinese General Su-ma Ch'ien, who lived around 100 BC: "The skillful employer of men will employ the wise man, the brave man, the covetous man and the stupid man. For the wise man delights in establishing his merit, the brave man likes to show his courage in action, the covetous man is quick at seizing advantages and the stupid man has no fear." Sounds like he played bridge.

A good player employs his forces (partners), too.

Start with a good player. Every game has a best player.

Let's call him The King. When you cut The King, put him to work for you. You know he has great skills; use those skills to your advantage. Don't try to impress him with your declarer play; instead, go out of your way to let him play the hand, or follow his line of defense, and respect his high-level decisions as you do his abilities. Compete fiercely for the partscores when he is your partner; his judgment will be good and he won't punish you. The best weapon in this partnership's arsenal is his talent, so don't let it be idle — put it to work like a general directing an army. Remember, "the wise man delights in establishing his merit."

But things are not the same when you are partnering the weakest player. First, remember that to get the best out of him you need to give him confidence and support. Next, remember that though his bridge game may be faulty, that doesn't make him a lesser human being. You owe him politeness and respect. If you need to attack your partner, wait till he's your opponent — and then "kill" him on the table with your superior play. But bridge-wise now your side is the underdog, so diplomatically, yet firmly, take over the reins, control the proceedings, and even hog the hand if necessary. Be conservative in the bidding, especially when he is going to be declarer. Look for plus scores, and settle for a small loss when a dangerous hand is dealt. A weak player made nervous or jittery is twice as dangerous than even his normal self.

There are many tactics to be learned for successfully *playing the table.* We saw an example of "taking the money" when bidding with a bad partner (by bidding four spades rather than four clubs or two diamonds). Here's one, relating to defense.

As you know, good players watch spot cards like hawks, while bad players see things more simply. To them there are big cards and small cards. You can make use of that. Playing with a weak player it's free to falsecard with small cards. You may lead the good opponent astray and your partner won't even notice what you're up to.

Here's an example of how you can "break the rules" when playing with a bad partner. It's rubber bridge, you're sitting West, and with neither side vulnerable, you pick up:

♠ K J 3 2 ♡ 7 6 4 ◇ 8 4 3 ♣ 9 6 2

One of these days you'll pick up better cards. Meanwhile, the auction goes:

	You		
South	West	North	East
1 NT*	pass	3 NT	(all pass)

1 NT = 15-17 points

What is your lead?

It certainly looks right to start with a spade, your only four-card suit. But if your partner is one who doesn't pay too close attention, you might try the effect of leading the ♠3 rather than the normal ♠2. The aim is to mislead the declarer into thinking that you have five spades.

A suitable layout might find declarer with this problem:

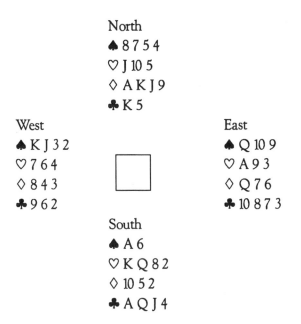

North
♠ 8 7 5 4
♡ J 10 5
◇ A K J 9
♣ K 5

West
♠ K J 3 2
♡ 7 6 4
◇ 8 4 3
♣ 9 6 2

East
♠ Q 10 9
♡ A 9 3
◇ Q 7 6
♣ 10 8 7 3

South
♠ A 6
♡ K Q 8 2
◇ 10 5 2
♣ A Q J 4

After you have led the ♠3 to the queen (declarer ducking) and your partner has led the ♠10 back (to the ace), declarer will be afraid that you may have the ♡A in addition to your supposed three good spades. He will try the diamond finesse to avoid giving you the lead, and will finish one down.

Remember, he thinks the spades were originally 5-2. He will think that even if the ◇Q is wrong, he will still make the contract when East has the ♡A.

If you had led the ♠2, declarer simply would have knocked out the ♡A.

This tactic can be equally effective the other way around, leading the fifth best from, say, ♠K-J-6-3-2.

God Save the Queen

There are many other techniques that are worthy of study. But there are also many *cards* worthy of care.

The queen of trumps is a precious card; learn to look after her.

Everybody knows that declarers take finesses in the play.

Very few know that defenders can take finesses in the bidding.

Playing for as high a stake as you can afford, sitting South, you pick up:

♠ A 10 9 8 7 ♡ K 2 ◊ K Q 6 4 ♣ 5 2

The auction races slamward like this:

			You
West	North	East	South
pass	1 ♣	3 ♡*	3 ♠
pass	4 ♡	pass	4 NT
pass	5 ♠	pass	5 NT
pass	6 ◊	pass	6 ♠
pass	pass	pass	

3 ♡ = preemptive overcall showing a seven-card suit and about 6-10 points.

West leads the ♡10, and this is what you survey:

North
♠ K J 6 3
♡ A 4
◊ A 5
♣ A J 10 8 3

☐

South (You)
♠ A 10 9 8 7
♡ K 2
◊ K Q 6 4
♣ 5 2

You can see a definite club loser, and there is a problem

in the trump suit. You win the heart lead in hand, cash the
♠A, everybody following, and lead a low spade toward the
dummy. When West plays the last low trump, do you finesse
or rise with the king? How's your nose?

While you're thinking about it, try this one. Once again
you are in six spades, with the same trump suit:

Dummy
♠ K J 6 3

Declarer
♠ A 10 9 8 7

This time you opened one spade. West, your left-hand
opponent, overcalled two notrump, the Unusual Notrump,
and your partner took over, driving you to the slam. Once
again you have a certain side-suit loser and the additional
problem of locating the ♠Q. How would you play the trump
suit?

In the first example, I'm sure you finessed West, the
partner of the three-heart preemptor, for the queen; and in
the second case you finessed East, the partner of the two-
notrump bidder. Most people would. Well done — at the
table you would have made both hands. Usually the odds
would be to cash the ace and king, trying to drop the queen.
However, following the preemptive bid, the odds change,
making the finesse a more attractive proposition.

But notice how both times a preempt became the signpost
for the declarer. As defenders, we all like to create problems
whenever possible, but we don't really want to give slams
away by helping declarers find the winning line of play.

If the declarer is going to play the partner of the preemptor
for the missing queen, maybe it's time the defense smartened

up and started preempting *with* the queen.

For example, non-vulnerable you pick up this hand:

♠ Q 4 ♡ K Q J 10 7 6 ◇ 8 3 2 ♣ 7 5

Your right-hand opponent opens one of a minor. Jump to three hearts. If the opponents play the hand, the queen of spades is likely to be a trick.

However, suppose you hold:

♠ 4 ♡ K Q J 10 7 6 ◇ 8 3 2 ♣ 7 5 2

Try the effect of overcalling with one heart rather than two hearts (weak) or three hearts (preemptive), which would normally be the correct bid with the weak hand. Then the opponents will play *you* for the points. Unless partner has a big hand, you will soon be defending. By making a simple overcall, you will be protecting your partner's key holdings, because the declarer will be playing *you* for the missing honor cards.

Similarly, suppose you hold either of these hands:

a) ♠ Q 4   b) ♠ 7 4
   ♡ 6   ♡ 6
   ◇ K Q J 10 7   ◇ K Q J 10 7
   ♣ K 10 9 6 3   ♣ K 10 9 6 3

If your RHO opens one heart or one spade, I much prefer a two-notrump overcall (unusual) on the first hand than on the second, with which I would simply overcall two diamonds. Protect the queen!

You can protect your partnership's trump holding in other ways. Have you faced this trump suit at the table?

44

Dummy
♠ K J 9 8

Declarer
♠ A 10 7 6

With no revealing bidding or play, declarer guesses the position of the queen half the time. How can we help him to do worse? Try to give him some rope — just enough to hang himself with. Here's how:

Opening Leads

With something to protect in the trump suit (either length or the queen), make your opening lead *as if it were* from a long suit. To declarer, this will imply shortness in the trump suit. Similarly, with shortness in the trumps, lead what *looks like* a short suit, protecting *partner's* trump stack.

Now for some examples. Sitting West, you pick up:

♠ Q 6 3   ♡ 10 9 2   ◊ 10 8 4 3   ♣ K 8 3

The auction is run-of-the-mill:

	You		
South	West	North	East
1 NT*	pass	2 ♣*	pass
2 ♠	pass	4 ♠	(all pass)

1 NT = 15-17 points
2 ♣ = Stayman

What is your lead?
Remember: Your aim is to try to protect your queen of trumps.

To imply diamond length, and therefore short trumps, lead the ◊ 3 (if playing third- and fifth-best leads), or the ◊ 4 if using fourth-best openings. Because of your supposed length in diamonds, declarer will "know" you have less room* for three trumps than your partner.

Against the same bidding, if you held this hand:

♠ 4 ♡ 9 8 2 ◊ Q 10 8 4 3 ♣ K J 10 2

you should lead the ♡8 or ♡9. Let declarer "know" that you have short hearts — and by implication, longer spades. Protect your partner's holdings!

The Singleton Switch

Sometimes fear can be a great weapon. Before he has drawn trumps, nothing scares declarer more than seeing a defender lead or switch to a singleton. The fear of a threatened ruff will normally cause declarer to draw trumps as quickly as possible, without the luxury of a finesse or safety play. However, what if you *haven't* been dealt a singleton? You have to make do with what you've been given!

Sitting East, you pick up this hand:

♠ Q 10 7 6 ♡ 10 2 ◊ 9 5 4 ♣ A 10 6 5

The bidding is simple:

---

* I am applying the Principle of Empty Spaces. Suppose you as declarer have to find the ♠Q in the last layout (K-J-9-8 opposite A-10-7-6). Unless the bidding has shown otherwise, it is 50-50 that (say) West will have Her Majesty. But if from the lead you deduce that, for example, West has five diamonds and East three, the odds change. There are only eight empty spaces in West's hand for the key queen, whereas there are 10 spaces in East's hand. It has become 5-to-4 odds that East holds the ♠Q.

	Partner		You
South	West	North	East
1 ♠	pass	2 ♡	pass
3 ♠	pass	4 ♠	(all pass)

Your partner leads the ♣K, and this is what you can see after the dummy has been tabled:

North
♠ 5 3
♡ A Q J 7 5
◊ K 7 6
♣ 9 4 3

East (You)
♠ Q 10 7 6
♡ 10 2
◊ 9 5 4
♣ A 10 6 5

♣K

The first trick goes like this: ♣K, 3, 6, 7.

Partner continues with the ♣2 to the 4, ace, jack.

You'd like to make two spade tricks to defeat the contract, but how can you stop declarer from finessing your ♠Q?

Switch to your singleton heart — and quickly!

You don't have a singleton heart? You know that, I know that, but *declarer* doesn't. If you switch to the ♡2, South is sure to win in the dummy, then bang down the ace and king of trumps to try to stop you from getting a heart ruff.

When he discovers your ruse, he'll either curse at you or ask you for a game, depending on his temperament.

This was the full deal:

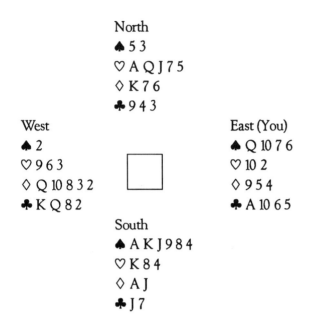

North
♠ 5 3
♡ A Q J 7 5
◊ K 7 6
♣ 9 4 3

West
♠ 2
♡ 9 6 3
◊ Q 10 8 3 2
♣ K Q 8 2

East (You)
♠ Q 10 7 6
♡ 10 2
◊ 9 5 4
♣ A 10 6 5

South
♠ A K J 9 8 4
♡ K 8 4
◊ A J
♣ J 7

You should realize that if you play a third club, declarer will ruff. Then he will cash one high spade, cross to dummy with a red suit, and finesse the ♠J, making the contract.

Doubling Cuebids

The opponents, on the way to a slam, have thrown in a cuebid. Often a defender will double the cuebid to direct the lead. That's as it should be. Also, the defender who doubles usually has *length* in the suit that he doubles.

As the actress said to the bishop, "Anything that helps declarer think you're long somewhere will also make him think you're short somewhere else."

When doubling, don't forget that. The next time the opponents are cuebidding their way to slam and you're looking at Q-x or Q-x-x of trumps, try doubling one of their cuebids, regardless of your holding in the suit, and quietly thank me afterward when you score your queen of trumps.

4

How to Be a Winner

Atlantic City, Monday Morning

Today the bridge would begin. People have different ways of preparing for a bridge match. There are those who rise early and go over their system with their partner. There are those who swim or jog, waking up their bodies. One of the players in Atlantic City had cycled for four days to get to the tournament — partly because of superstition and partly to clear his mind. There are even those who take pills, "pick me ups" and "pick me downs" — though they usually end up needing somebody else to pick up the pieces. There is another group to which I belong: the sleepers. The more I sleep, the happier I am. And the happier I am, the better I play — simple. I like to wake up as close to game time as possible. In my opinion, a tired mind is the most important thing to avoid. You need to be fully alert at every moment. It is one of the facts of bridge life that the one second you spend daydreaming will be the one when you make a mistake.

The only exception to this rule has been my recent interest in golf — a love strong enough to get me up early in the morning. Tim Holland, the golfer, was going to arrange a game for Tuesday. But this was Monday and the bridge game didn't start till 1 p.m., so I slept till noon. I ordered breakfast for 12:30 p.m., and I was in the playing area with a minute to spare.

"How are you feeling," asked a bleary-eyed Alan Sontag, my blackjack partner from the night before. He added, "You were smart to leave the game when you did; we all got killed."

Sympathetic, but glad that I had stopped, I grunted something in reply. The inquiry about how I was feeling wasn't just polite conversation. How I was feeling would be important. Playing well and feeling good go hand in hand.

Unlike regular events, where you enter as a pair or a team and play together throughout, here we were on our own, each entered as an individual. We would play only two hands in partnership with each of the other players in the field and then switch partners. The challenge would be great but different. Playing well in itself would not be enough. We would have to display adaptability as well as skill.

Let me discuss some of the main problems facing the competitors. Before playing the two deals, each partnership was given one minute to work out its methods. Although the number of permitted conventions was officially limited, this part could be tough. The players came from various countries with different schools of thought and different styles. So agreeing to a common system wasn't easy.

However, I considered it more important to know to which school of thought my partner belonged. For example, players from Europe, when defending, tend to signal count much more than Americans, who prefer to encourage or discourage — both methods quite different. Not knowing your partner's preference could cost a bushel of points.

Bidding methods, too, vary everywhere, even between the

east and west coasts of America. But rather than worry about individual bidding-system preferences, I preferred to know the individual characteristics of my partner. Was he cautious or aggressive? Was he a good declarer or defender? Modern or old-fashioned? Just knowing these things would be a huge advantage. But it was a lot to find out in one minute.

Some players are flexible, happy to play whatever makes their partners feel most comfortable. But others are stubborn, convinced that *their* way of playing is best. They hate to adjust from their type of game. That exactness is fine when playing with a regular partner, but was a disaster here. To win this tournament required a personality closer to the versatility of a chameleon than to the inflexibility of a martinet.

I had an advantage in that most people knew me. When I sat down to play, my partners wouldn't try to take charge of the hand in the fear that I was a weak player. This, more often than not, proves unsuccessful, but it would happen frequently to some of the foreign players, even the good ones, who were not known to their American partners. And although a top player's name may be well known, only a few recognize the face. Newspaper and magazine columns always carry bridge hands, rarely photographs.

This is where, I felt, I would have my biggest edge over the field. First, I knew nearly everybody because of my globetrotting. Second, my years of rubber bridge, learning the hard way to play with various styles, was by far the best training ground for an event like this — and for winning.

Winning means knowing a few tricks, arming yourself with the weapons of war. First, remember that circumstances change. People vary, and in this field it's necessary at times to improvise, compromise — even fraternize. Over the years I had learned the unwritten codes of rubber bridge. This would be the formula to follow. Here are my tips for getting the best results:

51

Partnering the Best Player (The King)
1. Never gloat over good results. Inevitably, the better your partnership, the more you will win.
2. Give him the opportunity to put his skills to work, i.e., let him play the hand.
3. Bid soundly so that he can rely on you.
4. Follow his defense whenever you are in any doubt.
5. Double the opponents more often — you can rely on getting the best defense.
6. Overbid on close situations when he is going to play the hand.
7. Don't be intimidated by him. He's your best friend.
8. Don't argue with him. The chances are that he's right.
9. "Pass" the crucial decision to him, especially at high levels, unless you know what to do.
10. Watch him and learn.

Playing with a Bad Partner (Godzilla)
1. Don't give him lessons. If he wanted them, he'd go to a bridge school.
2. Avoid the possibility of accidents; a small profit is better than a big loss. Don't go for the best possible result; the best result possible should be your target.
3. Learn his style, and compensate for an over- or under-bidder. Are his penalty doubles sound? If so, leave them in.
4. Bid simply; and go out of your way to indicate the right lead.
5. Take control; make the key decisions for him, even when technically this isn't the best approach. Hog the hand.
6. Give very loud signals in defense; give him signposts to follow.
7. Falsecard with low cards to fool the good player; your partner isn't watching anyway.
8. Protect him from tough opponents, building a fence — even a trap — around him.

9. If you must lose, do it gracefully.

10. Try harder; don't give up just because you're the underdog.

Playing against the Bad Partner (Godzilla)

1. Give him leeway on revokes, bids out of turn, exposed cards. You want to beat him, not murder him — and you have enough advantages already.

2. Never forget that he is going to be your partner in the next rubber.

3. Bad players expect to go down and give up easily, so make a penalty double at the slightest excuse when he is playing the hand.

4. Allow him to make mistakes; don't get in the way.

5. Understand his style and use it against him. For example, compete more if he doesn't double.

6. Give him high-level decisions. You know he has poor judgment, so let him use it.

7. Play honor cards through him. He'll always cover if he can.

8. Signal on defense as much as you like to your partner when Godzilla is declarer — he won't be watching.

9. Keep him on lead, he'll probably find the wrong one.

10. Push him around at the partscore level.

The understanding of yourself is quite as important as any of these tips. It isn't easy to do, but if you can find certain inconsistencies, strengths or weaknesses in your character, you can accentuate the positive and eliminate, or work around, the negative. For example, suppose that you are cautious by nature. The next time you are resolving a close decision, take the aggressive course — which leads us to the next subject matter: penalty doubles.

To Double or Not To Double

The most underused weapon by good and bad players alike is the penalty double. Not just *underused*, but also *abused* and *misused*. In the old days, if Ali Baba wanted riches, he said, "Open Sesame." Today, "Double" works just as well. It's time to stop playing like a chicken — get out your gun and start doubling.

The first question is: *Whom* do you double?

The answer: *everybody* — good and bad players alike. Let's start with the bad. Remember:

1. Fact number one: The world is overflowing with bad bridge players.
2. Fact number two: Bad bridge players love to go down, given the slightest excuse.
3. Fact number three: When doubled, a bad player finds it impossible to think clearly. Also, he is so sure that the cards lie badly and that he must now go down, he's almost relieved that he won't be failing in a hand that he should have made.

The second question is: *When* do you double?

The answer: whenever the bad player is going to be declarer and any one of the following exists:

1. Any key suit, *especially* trumps, is breaking badly, particularly when the auction has revealed that they have no extra values.
2. When the bad player is obviously stretching.

You			Bad Player
West	North	East	South
—	pass	pass	1 NT
pass	2 NT	pass	3 NT*

or

Bad Player	You		
South	West	North	East
1 ♠	pass	2 ♠	pass
3 ♠*	pass	4 ♠	

* Made after some thought, which nearly always means he's on the borderline between passing and bidding on.

3. When you want to suggest a lead.
4. You don't like the "sound" of the bidding — or you just feel mean.

Here is an example from actual play. Sitting East, you pick up this hand:

♠ 7 4 ♡ A J ◊ K 10 9 7 4 ♣ J 9 5 2

The bidding proceeds like this:

Bad Player			You
South	West	North	East
pass	pass	1 ◊	pass
1 ♡	pass	2 ♡	pass
4 ♡	pass	pass	double

The double was based on this thinking: The contract is bound to be close (South is a passed hand, and North bid only two hearts). A spade or club lead may give away a trick — a diamond lead looks best. The more you double, the more you win. West led the ◊8. This was the full deal:

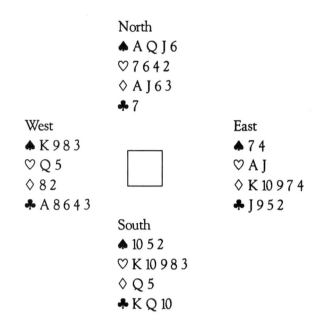

North
♠ A Q J 6
♡ 7 6 4 2
◊ A J 6 3
♣ 7

West
♠ K 9 8 3
♡ Q 5
◊ 8 2
♣ A 8 6 4 3

East
♠ 7 4
♡ A J
◊ K 10 9 7 4
♣ J 9 5 2

South
♠ 10 5 2
♡ K 10 9 8 3
◊ Q 5
♣ K Q 10

The play was interesting and amusing. East won the first trick with the ◊K, then returned the ◊10 to South's queen. The declarer led the ♣Q; West won with the ace and switched to the *nine* of spades, suggesting no spade honor. Fooled by this good play, declarer panicked and called for dummy's ♠A, then led a heart from dummy. East rose with the ace, led a spade to his partner's king, received a spade ruff, and then led a diamond. This effected a trump promotion for the ♡Q — three down and plus 800 to East-West.

I know that declarer misplayed by two(!) tricks. He should certainly finesse the ♠Q. But that's exactly what happens when you double a bad player. Finally, note that on a spade lead (probable without the double) declarer actually would have made his contract. Psychological doubles may be theoretically unsound, but in practice they are very rewarding.

You can catch a good player, too, with these slightly speculative doubles — especially when he's partnered with a bad player. All you need to do is listen to the bidding. Take the following auction:

You	Bad Player	Partner	Good Player
West	North	East	South
—	—	pass	1 ♡
1 ♠	2 ♡	2 ♠	3 ♡*
3 ♠	4 ♡*	pass	pass
double*			

3 ♡ = When a good player bids three hearts, he has judged his side cannot make game. (Three hearts by a good player in this sort of sequence is purely competitive. He would bid a new suit if he were interested in partner's cooperation in trying to bid a game.)

4 ♡ = The bad player makes the impossible and wrong bid for the thousandth time.

double = Don't look at your hand — punish them. Trust the good player's judgment. If *he* didn't think he could make four hearts, why should you?

Getting Doubled

Do you dread being doubled? "Yes," you say. Would it surprise you to learn that on occasions I love it? Actually sometimes I try very hard to get doubled. Yes, you heard me. After reading this, so will you.

Have you ever held a bad hand like:

♠ Q 10 9 5 4 2 ♡ 2 ◇ J 10 9 2 ♣ 9 2 ?

You hear your partner open one notrump (12-14 points), and your right-hand opponent doubles. You bid two spades, happy to have a safe port in a storm.

If you agree that the opponents probably have a game somewhere, next time you might decide to try a friendly psych in this position. Bid two clubs or even two hearts. The opponents will double, and then you run to two spades. Yes, it's probable they will now shrug off your little joke and bid their game. But sometimes — just sometimes — they will miscalculate and double you, which is what you were angling for. Put it another way: What can you lose?

However, remember two points: (1) Don't do this on every occasion, because the opponents soon get wise; (2) make the psychic bid in a lower-ranking suit than the real one, just in case partner takes you back to your first suit — at least you can correct at the same level.

Bidding a short suit can work, too. You're West at favorable vulnerability, holding:

♠ 10 9 6 4   ♡ 8 5 3   ◊ K 9 8 4 3   ♣ 7

West	North	East	South
—	1 NT	2 NT*	4 ♡
?			

2 NT = unusual; a minor two-suiter.

What do you bid?

Your thoughts should run along these lines: It's their hand. You know you would like to play in five diamonds (doubled). If you bid five diamonds directly, it's unlikely you'll be allowed to play there. A bid of five clubs will attract a double. Then a run-out to five diamonds might induce a rhythm double, your opponents thinking you are floundering. Try this sometime; you'll be surprised how often it works.

I suppose I have Godzilla to thank for learning this strategy. I still remember the hand. It was during the late-night game at Stefan's. I had just cut the Apeman against two fair players. Already smelling blood, they were like a pair of hungry Dobermans, straining at their leashes, ready to attack. Worse, I picked up this hand:

♠ — ♡ 5 4 2 ◇ Q J 10 7 6 ♣ 10 9 5 4 3

I'm not usually a coward, but cutting Godzilla and holding this hand is enough to scare anybody. Trouble loomed. Worse, he grunted out one spade. The next hand overcalled two hearts. Now it was my call. Already with visions of being dummy in five or six spades doubled with a 5-0 fit, I started thinking of ways to get out of my impending predicament.

These seemed to be my options:

1. I could double the opponents in a partscore — they might not redouble and the loss would be cheaper than the penalty about to hit us.

2. I could make an insufficient bid, then change it, barring Godzilla from further action. But that is unethical; and anyway these opponents were smart enough to waive the penalty just to let him keep bidding.

3. A bit drastic, I could resort to a violent solution. Suicide and murder were both possibilities — if slightly premature.

Eventually, I decided just to pass and the bidding continued:

Godzilla		Zia	
South	West	North	East
1 ♠	2 ♡	pass	2 ♠*
?			

2 ♠ = usually a good high-card heart raise — a stronger bid than an immediate bid of three or four hearts.

At this point, my partner started to think. The more he thought, the more I sweated. How many spades was he going to bid? When he finally made up his mind, his bid both surprised and delighted me. He said, "Four diamonds." Mentally, I apologized for doubting him.

Godzilla		Zia	
South	West	North	East
1 ♠	2 ♡	pass	2 ♠*
4 ◊	4 ♡	?	

But now I had a new problem. When my right-hand opponent bid four hearts, I wanted to raise to five diamonds, but these opponents would realize that I'd never raise Godzilla to the five-level unless I had a real mountain. No, that would be a complete giveaway. They would surely bid five hearts. I needed to find a way to buy the hand in five diamonds doubled. Any ideas?

I bid four spades! The prospect of Godzilla playing in four spades when East was looking at five trumps was too much for him. He barked out a double. This was passed back to me, and I retreated immediately to five diamonds. Once more, a resounding double. This was the full deal:

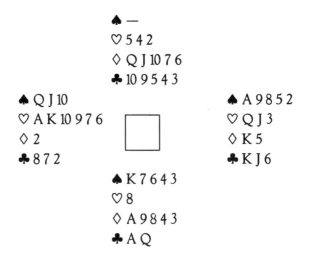

```
                    ♠ —
                    ♡ 5 4 2
                    ◊ Q J 10 7 6
                    ♣ 10 9 5 4 3
  ♠ Q J 10                        ♠ A 9 8 5 2
  ♡ A K 10 9 7 6                  ♡ Q J 3
  ◊ 2                             ◊ K 5
  ♣ 8 7 2                         ♣ K J 6
                    ♠ K 7 6 4 3
                    ♡ 8
                    ◊ A 9 8 4 3
                    ♣ A Q
```

Not even the great ape could find a way to go down. I was full of praise, carefully not to point out that he could have made an overtrick.

5

The Sting

Mike, yesterday's puzzler, appeared suddenly. "Will you let me off the dinner I owe you if I give you some really good news?"

He will do *anything* to avoid losing a bet! But for me it was at least a no-loss situation, so I agreed.

"You're going to be in the *pit* for the qualifying rounds," he informed me.

Better — that really suited me. In some tournaments a "pit" is set up to enable spectators to watch without disturbing the players or crowding on top of each other. This consists of a table set apart from the others around which chairs are placed in ascending rows, rather like a mini-football stadium. In this way more people can watch in comfort for all — themselves and the players. I had been allocated the stationary position in the pit. Players would come to my table, play their hands and leave. I would remain seated.

Why was it good news? For several reasons. Whereas some

players become nervous at having too many spectators, others prefer it. Personally I love it. The showman in me somehow performs better when I am playing to a gallery. Second, the spectators will normally root for the stationary player, although their support is, of course, not vocal. Their well-wishes would be obvious and would make me the equivalent of the *home team*. Third, the fact that I wouldn't have to keep moving around, looking for the table, meant I would have more time to discuss my methods with my new partners — certainly a bonus.

The tournament would last four days, from Monday to Thursday. Everyone would play for two days, after which the field would be cut to 40 players for the two-day final. There was a consolation event for those who didn't make the final.

Because the carryover of points from the qualifying stage (the first two days) was small, the goal for those days was just to qualify; the main tactic was to play "down the middle," avoiding disasters. Once in the final, it would be time to use the whip and be more aggressive.

The scoring was by international match points (imps), where the emphasis is on beating or making contracts and not taking risks by trying to make overtricks. It is like rubber bridge rather than pairs.

Once everyone was seated, the tournament director explained the movement and conditions of contest. There was pin-drop silence — the announcements were important and everyone listened intently. Each player reacts differently to this stage of the tournament. There are those, even experienced players, who feel tense and tight, sitting in silence until they feel the reassurance of the cards in their hands. Others can joke and talk, outwardly relaxed but inwardly readying themselves for the mental effort ahead. And it *is* an effort. The strain on a top expert's mind while he is in a tournament is incredible. I saw a survey that found that the level of concentration of a bridge expert is as intense as that of a brain surgeon in the operating theater. The problems and vital points of bridge hands come up at any time; it is easy to miss the key moment, only to regret it bitterly a few seconds later.

It is possible to relax only when you are the dummy, although even that can be difficult. There is one woman who has won several world championships who knits between hands, resting and recharging her batteries after bouts of intense concentration.

As the director finished giving his instructions, the familiar hum of conversation restarted. Boards of duplicated pre-dealt hands were being placed on the tables. Then a voice came over the public address system: "Game time!"

The session started well and luckily for me. My first partner was Mike Passell, one of the very best American players. He is a professional "hired gun" and ex-world champion. He is built like an American football player and plays as tough as he looks. Sitting South, he picked up this hand:

♠ A Q 6 4 3 ♡ 9 6 2 ◇ A Q 5 ♣ A Q

The bidding proceeded:

Passell		*Zia*	
South	West	North	East
1 ♠	pass	2 ♠	pass
3 ♡*	pass	4 ♠	(all pass)

3 ♡ = in principle, a game-try, asking for help in hearts, though it very well could be a natural suit.

This was the full hand:

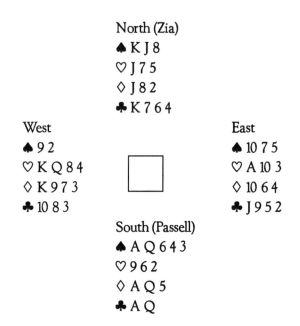

North (Zia)
♠ K J 8
♡ J 7 5
♢ J 8 2
♣ K 7 6 4

West
♠ 9 2
♡ K Q 8 4
♢ K 9 7 3
♣ 10 8 3

East
♠ 10 7 5
♡ A 10 3
♢ 10 6 4
♣ J 9 5 2

South (Passell)
♠ A Q 6 4 3
♡ 9 6 2
♢ A Q 5
♣ A Q

Once I responded two spades, Passell had every intention of going to game, but on the way there he stopped off to bid three hearts. He wanted to avoid a heart lead, which looked the most dangerous. So he took a little insurance: He bid the suit!

It worked when West decided to protect his heart holding and led a spade instead. Passell won in hand, unblocked the ♣A-Q, drew trumps ending in the dummy, and discarded a heart loser on the ♣K. He lost one diamond and two heart tricks. Plus 420 was a great score.

That three-heart bid is the kind of action that costs nothing and often turns out to be very effective. Surprisingly, it is hardly used by anyone. You don't need to be a genius to make the strategy work for you. A heart lead defeats four spades, and that lead was made at most tables where the bidding went: one spade-two spades-four spades. I thanked Passell, who smiled in acknowledgment. It would have been bad manners to rub it in to our deflated opponents — bad tactics, too, for the players now switched around and an opponent became my partner.

Let's take another look at this bidding tactic.

The words "the sting" probably make you think of Paul Newman and Robert Redford, and "the sting" is actually an expression used by the underworld to describe a "con" — a kind of artistic thievery. Passell's phony game-try is a tactic among experts, the bridge equivalent of the sting. There are three common types of this deception: Sting Game-Tries, Sting Cuebids and Sting Splinters.

Sting Game-Tries

Try this hand from a recent money game. You are West, holding:

♠ J 5 4   ♡ Q 7 2   ◇ 10 9 6   ♣ A Q 10 9

South	West	North	East
1 ♠	pass	2 ♠	pass
3 ♣	pass	4 ♠	(all pass)

What do you lead? Think about that for a moment.

Suppose you have a big hand and the auction starts like this:

You	LHO	Partner	RHO
1 Major	pass	2 Major	pass
?			

Partner has raised your major-suit opening. Before you bid on, *think*. If you intend to bid game, but can see that a particular lead may be dangerous, consider trying to dissuade the opponents from leading that suit by bidding the suit on the way to game.

Sometimes you can even direct a favorable lead. Say you have a hand like this:

♠ J 10 9 5 4 ♡ A Q 4 ◊ A Q 7 ♣ A K

After partner raises one spade to two spades, you can see that a diamond or heart lead may well give you a trick. It costs nothing to bid three clubs to encourage the opponents to be a little friendly.

Now back to the lead problem. A trump looks right — you might have a lot of club winners if they aren't ruffed in the dummy. This is sound thinking, but expensive — a clever South has just "stung" you. This was the full hand:

North (LHO)
♠ K 3 2
♡ J 6 5
◊ J 7 3
♣ K 8 6 5

West (You)
♠ J 5 4
♡ Q 7 2
◊ 10 9 6
♣ A Q 10 9

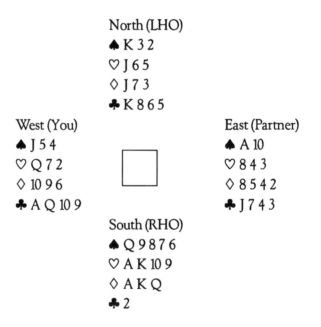

East (Partner)
♠ A 10
♡ 8 4 3
◊ 8 5 4 2
♣ J 7 4 3

South (RHO)
♠ Q 9 8 7 6
♡ A K 10 9
◊ A K Q
♣ 2

South, who always intended to bid four spades after his partner's raise, could see possible trump problems ahead. It would be nice if he could persuade West to lead a trump. But how?

By bidding his short suit, where West was likely to have strength and a desire to protect his tricks before they were ruffed away.

You don't need to be Garozzo to make such bids. The concept is simple enough for even the local palooka to soon master the theory. All you need is a little bit of larceny in your heart. However, I have a word of warning. If you use these ploys regularly at duplicate with your partner, you must inform the opponents about your style.

Bridge is a funny game. Stealing is encouraged, but holding back information is totally taboo.

Sting Cuebids

You've been losing all afternoon. Worse, the opponents have announced that this is to be the last rubber (they always seem to be in a rush when they're winning). You're steaming (trying to catch up), but at last you pick up an opening bid:

♠ A Q J 3 ♡ K 5 ◇ 8 7 3 ♣ A 6 5 3

The bidding starts like this (no opposing bidding):

Partner	You
1 ♡	1 ♠
3 ♠	?

At this point, a slam looks likely. What's more, your bank balance needs it. But what do you bid?

These are the apparent possibilities: four clubs (a cuebid, hoping to hear four diamonds), four notrump (checking up on aces), or six spades (a reasonable bash).

But I don't bid any of these! Think ahead.

You're scared of a diamond lead, but just in time you realize you're more scared of going home and admitting to your losses. You need to make a slam to avoid a row at home.

You try to stop the diamond lead and you *sting* with a four-diamond cuebid. With a bit of luck and no diamond lead you might catch a dummy like this:

♠ K 10 8 4 ♡ A Q J 10 9 ◇ Q 2 ♣ K Q

The opponents may not fall for it next time, but that's next time — when you'll make the *genuine* cuebid of four clubs!

Look for the opportunity to make phony cuebids — they come up all the time.

Sting Splinters

This one is for tournament players who are looking for a way to engineer a coup. Rubber-bridge players may not be able to use it.

A splinter bid (usually a double jump to show a fit for partner and shortness in the bid suit) is very useful. It is clear, concise and quick. It carries a lot of information, but it also helps the opponents as well as your partner. Suppose, as North, you hold:

♠ A J 10 4 ♡ A 7 6 ◇ 3 ♣ A K Q 10 6

You open the bidding with one club. Partner responds one spade. With no opposition bidding, it comes back to you. What do you bid?

A splinter of four diamonds is the normal action, which may get you to a magic slam. However, it also pinpoints to your opponents the heart lead that may defeat four or six spades. Occasionally you might wish to consider the alternative of a phoney splinter: three hearts (or four hearts). This will attract a diamond lead, which may be vital.

Partner could have any one of these:

	(a)		(b)		(c)
	♠ K Q 7 6		♠ Q 9 5 3		♠ K 9 7 5 2
	♡ K Q 3		♡ 9 5 4		♡ J 2
	◊ 9 7 4		◊ K Q 6		◊ A 5 2
	♣ 7 5 4		♣ J 8 2		♣ 8 7 2

With hand (a), the phoney splinter will backfire. Looking at the supposed losers in diamonds, partner will sign off in four spades, whereas if you had made the normal splinter of four diamonds, you might have reached the magic slam. Nothing works all the time!

However, with hand (b), the four-diamond splinter attracts the feared heart lead. Now four spades goes one down if the trump finesse loses. After the four-heart splinter and a diamond lead, four spades make plus 450 (or 480 when the spade finesse wins.)

Finally, with hand (c), both splinters get you to the slam, but after a heart lead, your back is against the wall, hoping for some luck in the trump suit. But after a diamond lead, you're practically lay-down.

Save one of these bids for a rainy day when you want to *live a little*. It's a killer when it comes off. But people are getting so used to my coming up with this sort of craziness that if I make one of these bids, my opponents don't trust me. You, on the other hand, have probably got some time ahead before they wise up. So go ahead — *sting* a little.

London

I'm often asked how long it took me to learn to play well. That is a tough question. I suppose it was about two years before I felt I was ready to play against the best, but that was two years of playing daily, often 10 to 12 hours at a stretch.

Ten to 12 hours at a bridge table is unlike 10 to 12 hours anywhere else. To say that time flies would be an understatement. "Disappears" would be more accurate. At Stefan's, when Dr. Manch, one of the most successful players at the club, was told how well I was doing in the lower-stake games, he always said, "He's just lucky. Wait until he gets to my table. Then we'll show him how to play bridge."

When I finally arrived at the big table, I learned that winning can have its drawbacks. Stefan would calculate the total of the cheques of the players who "knocked" (defaulted) after they lost to the expert. I must have been pretty hot because it wasn't long before Stefan gave me the dubious honor of stopping me from playing — including at Manch's table — except on rare occasions.

"You're too good," he would say. "You'll ruin my business."

The comment stroked my ego, but to be the best money player in a club was a long way from being a top internationalist. It was time to try the tournament world.

Paradise

If you sat on your magic carpet in May and told it to take you to Paradise, it would head straight for the South of France. The sun shines, but not enough to burn; the beaches have bodies, but not unwelcome crowds — and that's only the *aperitif.*

The natural beauty of the country, the contrast between the blue of the Mediterranean and the splendor of the mountains, is superb, enough to enthrall even the most urban of tastes. Any visitor whose resistance is still not overcome by this would then be happily seduced by the best food on earth. Bouillabaisse, the fish soup, which is a specialty of the Côte d'Azur, is wonderful beyond description. And it is matched by the fabulous cooking of any of the restaurants that you just come across accidentally while exploring the region: La Chaumiere, Villefranche, or Têtu in Antibes.

The French are brilliant — I say that because every year for a month or so in spring they hold a series of bridge tournaments on the Côte d'Azur. The locations include holiday resorts such as Juan-les-Pins, Cannes and Monte

Carlo. Unlike bridge tournaments in most countries (especially America), these are holidays first and bridge events second — with only one session of play a day. This is one reason why bridge is thriving in France. The games start at three or four in the afternoon and end at seven or eight — enough to whet your appetite but not enough to drown you.

Having decided to try the world of tournament bridge, my initial sortie was here, to the South of France. Teaming up with Martin Hoffman, a regular visitor to the continent, my first stop was Juan-les-Pins. If you have to go to school, there's no harm going to one where they serve champagne with breakfast and where the discotheques never close.

The tournaments vary in length, and beginners and experts are both equally welcome and equally in evidence. The one in Juan lasts 14 days. There are four events, the Individual, the Mixed Pairs, the Open Pairs and the Teams. You can enter as many or as few as you like.

We had arrived too late for the Individual. Let me tell you about the Mixed. For most players, a mixed pairs (with the exception of world championships) is a social outing. But there is an art in doing well. Often the field is full of unbalanced partnerships with one better player (man or woman) playing under sufferance with his or her mate. It is a mutant form of the game, where the senior partners try to hog all the hands and bid as if playing solo or cut-throat. But all the while they are trying to disguise what they are doing in order to retain their partner's dignity. It isn't easily done, which helps explain the violent fights, tears and shattered illusions — even broken marriages.

My idea of action during the two days of the Mixed was to browse lazily through a good book on the beach, with the occasional exercise of reaching out for a nearby cocktail. And that's exactly what I was doing when Hoffman came running up just half an hour before the start of the session. He said, "I've found you a partner for the Mixed."

"What on earth are you talking about? You know I have no intention . . . "

My reply was interrupted by Martin. "Here she is."

I looked up. There are very few things that could have dragged me away from my idyllic resting-place and made me change my original plan. Monique just happened to be one of them. With sparkling green eyes and a soft, throaty voice, Monique was almost unreal. The closest I can get to describing her is to compare the feeling one gets from picking up a 10-card suit for the first time — a mixture of fantasy fulfilled and the surge of wild expectation. All in all, she was impossible to resist. Doubtless, she couldn't play, but who would be watching her cards?

Bridge is a pure game, cerebral and intellectually satisfying. I think it is inappropriate, even disgusting, for one person to play with another simply because he finds her physically attractive. But what could I do? I admit it — I am disgusting. Anyway, Monique wasn't just attractive, she was a knockout.

Things didn't go well. In fact, the first day's game was a disaster. We were lying 180th out of a possible 190. It was caused by nervousness (Monique), bad luck and lust (me). Monique was close to tears at the end of play and rushed off. My dinner plans were ruined. I couldn't help thinking that this was no way to impress her.

Born out of the threat of frustrated romance, great ideas can sometimes emerge. So was born "Le Pique Pakistani" (the Paki Spade): a system designed to bring the smile back to Monique's charming face and — hopefully — the love back to my life.

The theory was simple enough. Whenever we were nonvulnerable and it was our turn to open the bidding, we would call one spade — regardless of strength and distribution. Partner could be scientific and respond one notrump with a good hand of 13-plus points as a kind of "what have you got?" bid; or otherwise just play it by ear, trying to cause as much havoc as possible. After all, we couldn't do any worse!

We declared our system to our opponents, of course, and then *Jackpot!* The element of surprise, luck, fate, whatever — I don't really know — but good results poured in as the opponents succumbed to the devilishness of the system.

Here is an example:

North dealer
East-West vulnerable

North (Zia)
♠ 6 4
♡ A Q J 9 3
◊ Q 9 4
♣ 7 6 3

West
♠ K Q 10 5
♡ 8 2
◊ J 3
♣ A Q 8 5 4

East
♠ A J 9 7
♡ K 7 6
◊ K 10 6
♣ J 9 2

South (Monique)
♠ 8 3 2
♡ 10 5 4
◊ A 8 7 5 2
♣ K 10

West	North	East	South
—	1 ♠ (1)	pass (2)	2 ♠! (3)
pass (4)	3 ♡	(all pass)	

(1) The Paki Spade
(2) Stuck.
(3) Take that!
(4) S(t)ucker.

73

The opponents could have made four or five spades, rather luckily. But it was difficult for them to get to four spades when not only one but *both* opponents had bid spades. (Fifteen years later a similar but more refined method of destruction was devised in New Zealand, following its original invention in Poland. "Fert" bids were inflicted on the bridge world — where opening bids of one diamond, one heart or one spade, depending upon vulnerability, would show 0-7 points. The "fert" moniker is an abbreviation for fertilizer, so named because the bids are intended to aid the growth of good results.) Le Pique Pakistani was before its time.

The upshot was that we moved up 140 places, finishing a respectable 40th.

Monique was delighted.

I was delighted that Monique was delighted.

And the love affair?

I suppose you could say that we celebrated our success in the usual manner.

* * * * * * * * *

If I thought the transition from rubber bridge to duplicate would be easy, I soon learned otherwise. The rest of the tournament was undistinguished for me as far as results were concerned. But this just helped to bring home some of the fundamental differences between rubber and tournament bridge.

Rubber bridge is a jungle where survival comes first. You are on your own, and the emphasis is on improvisation and adaptability. In the final analysis, the key to success is doing the right thing to suit the conditions. Your individual instinct and ability are your weapons. The tournament world, in contrast, is closer to an arena, where well-trained and well-armed gladiators fight. The key is to succeed through better preparation, and by functioning as an efficient unit with your partner. They are different games, and both offer their own types of equally pleasurable satisfaction. I would say that rubber is more "human," while the tournament game is more "pure," closer to par, and where methods take the place of judgment and guesswork.

To give you an example, from the same tournament in Juan-les-Pins, the following situation took place. North opened one notrump (strong). The next player, East, had this hand:

♠ K 3 ♡ A Q 10 4 ◇ 6 ♣ K Q 10 9 8 3

In a rubber-bridge game you would overcall two clubs and play there. But in duplicate the two-club overcall is rarely used in this natural way.

Tournament players have methods to deal with hands like this. East bid a conventional two clubs, showing *hearts* and another suit. West's hand was:

♠ 7 6 4 2 ♡ K 9 8 3 ◇ 8 7 5 2 ♣ A

Now four hearts was easy to reach, West jumping to three hearts and East going on to game. As you can see, having an understanding or method to deal with a particular situation can be more useful than any amount of skill.

Cannes

After Juan we drove down the coast to Cannes.

Cannes: Movie stars, the Carlton Hotel, lobster, Goulash (a form of bridge popular in France in which the cards aren't shuffled, leading to voids and nine-card suits becoming everyday occurrences), and a tournament shorter in duration than Juan's. We did slightly better, finishing in the money. I liked the tournament, and have returned regularly over the years. The best result I ever had there was in 1988 while playing with the brilliant young Indian player Jaggy Shivdasani — though it was almost a disaster. But before describing that incident, what was I, a Pakistani, doing playing with an Indian, the traditional enemy?

I don't know — put it down to just another instance of the way in which bridge doesn't seem to allow people to know or care where they come from. It is impervious to society's traditional barriers of age, color, religion or beliefs. Put it down to the magic, the spell that the game mysteriously weaves, bewitching all those who come into contact with it.

This was Jaggy's first trip to the South of France. A very talented player, whose enthusiasm at the table is a reflection of his attitude to life, he is the text-book tourist, always ready with his camera to go on any excursion. He bubbles excitedly through life.

We had an enormous session of 70 percent on the first day of the Open Pairs. This is the equivalent of scoring a hat-trick of goals; and we were leading the field. It was about one in the afternoon on the final day's play. I was where I belonged, blissfully asleep, when the phone rang.

"*Help*," a voice screamed.

"Excuse me," I muttered, still drowsy. I wasn't reacting too well.

"Help me, I'm stuck."

At last I recognized Jaggy's voice. He went on to explain that he had gone on a boat excursion to an island off the coast. Busy clicking away, engrossed in using up rolls of film, he had misunderstood the departure point; he was in time to see the boat sailing away. The next boat wasn't due until 3 p.m., which was also the time the game was due to start. This meant he would be at least half an hour late.

Jaggy was on the verge of winning his first international tournament and fate had stranded him on an island five miles away. He was desperate, and he pleaded with me to hire a boat to save him.

"Do something, wake up, get up, go to the dock and pay a fisherman to sail out and rescue me," he pleaded. "But look for one with an old boat. That might be cheaper," he added as an afterthought.

Where was I going to find a sympathetic French fisherman prepared to rescue a bridge playing Indian savage who was marooned on a not-so-desert island? Just trying to explain the predicament in my limited French was likely to get me locked up. And it's a fact that most Frenchmen refuse to speak English even if they can understand it. I seriously contemplated going back to sleep. I was probably dreaming anyway.

On the other hand, as far as I knew, this was the first time that a Pakistani and an Indian had ever teamed up in international competition — it would be a great bonus if we won. I tried this line on the concierge, but, sadly, this appeal to a higher ideal was totally wasted on him. He did react sympathetically to a 200-franc note and promised to make enquiries, which naturally proved to be fruitless.

As a last resort, I appealed to the highest authority: the Tournament Director. I was ready with my pathetic story of the dangers of traveling in a foreign land. He was surprisingly understanding and agreed sportingly to give us a maximum half an hour's grace during which I could play with a substitute. I told Jaggy this when he called back, adding a few choice descriptions of my views about his lineage, using some of the words that are common to both Urdu (the Pakistani language) and Hindi (the Indian language).

Nines

The story had a happy ending. Jaggy managed to make it before the deadline, and, though physically slightly the worse for wear, his bridge skills were not dimmed. I remember a great hand he played, but first some instruction, some advice that may seem out of the Twilight Zone. In defense, every time you have a nine, think about playing it at the first opportunity.

You read me; stay with me, I'm not crazy!

Most people know that they should (although they never do) play the nine in these positions:

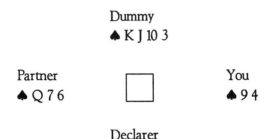

Dummy
♠ K J 10 3

Partner   You
♠ Q 7 6   [ ]   ♠ 9 4

Declarer
♠ A 8 5 2

Declarer cashes the ace: *drop the nine.*

Dummy
♡ J 8 6 3

You   Partner
♡ 10 9 2   ♡ Q 5

Declarer
♡ A K 7 4

When declarer cashes the ace, *play the nine.* Declarer may now cross to dummy and call for the jack, which caters both to a singleton 9 and wins big if you started with the 10-9 doubleton. Or he may lead low from his hand, toward dummy, on the second round.

Dummy
◊ K Q 10 5

You   Partner
◊ J 9 6 4   ◊ 3

Declarer
◊ A 8 7 2

When declarer leads low toward the dummy, put in the 9. Declarer will probably cash the queen next, playing your partner for ◊ J-6-4-3.

Dummy
♣ Q 10 8 5 4

Partner   You
♣ J 7 2   ♣ K 9 3

Declarer
♣ A 6

Play the 9 under the ace. Declarer's "correct" play now is low to the queen.

In all these situations, playing the nine cannot cost, and may win a trick. If nothing else, it keeps declarer under pressure.

How about this one:

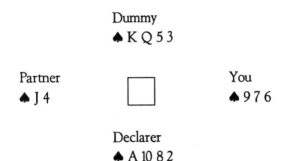

Dummy
♠ K Q 5 3

Partner
♠ J 4

You
♠ 9 7 6

Declarer
♠ A 10 8 2

Left to his own devices, declarer will start with the king, then the queen. However, if you play the 9 under the king, he will cross to the *ace* at the second trick, allowing for your having a singleton. This may be useful if you want him to use up a hand entry prematurely. Playing the 9 can transfer the tempo of playing a suit from the declarer to the defenders. For example:

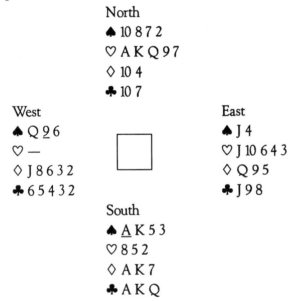

North
♠ 10 8 7 2
♡ A K Q 9 7
♢ 10 4
♣ 10 7

West
♠ Q 2 6
♡ —
♢ J 8 6 3 2
♣ 6 5 4 3 2

East
♠ J 4
♡ J 10 6 4 3
♢ Q 9 5
♣ J 9 8

South
♠ A K 5 3
♡ 8 5 2
♢ A K 7
♣ A K Q

South arrived at six spades, and West led the ♣6. Declarer won in hand and cashed the ♠A. If West had followed with the 6, declarer would have had no option but to play for trumps to break 3-2. However, when West followed with the 9, declarer played "safe" by leading a low trump out of his hand in case East started with four spades. In this case that led to disaster. East won with the ♠J and gave his partner a heart ruff.

The nine can work overtime — not many people are aware of the following positions in notrump contracts:

Dummy
♡ 4

West   East
♡ K 8 7 2   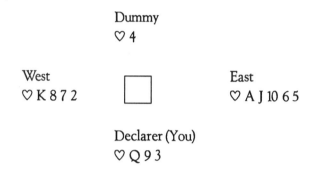   ♡ A J 10 6 5

Declarer (You)
♡ Q 9 3

Your left-hand opponent leads the 2; because you have the 9, you can block the suit. If East wins with the ace and returns the jack, you cover with the queen. West has to win the fourth round of the suit. Alternatively, if East returns the 5 or 6, the 9 prevents the defense from taking the obvious five tricks.

Dummy
◊ Q 9 2

West   East
◊ K 10 8 7   ◊ A J 6 5 4

Declarer (You)
◊ 3

West leads the 7. You insert the 9 to hold them to four immediate tricks.

So treat the nine with respect; use it to terrify and mislead declarers. Start throwing it around even if you're not always sure why.

Jaggy must share my views; watch him in action:

South dealer
North-South vulnerable

North
♠ A 5 3
♡ K 8 4
◇ J 8 6 3
♣ K 10 4

West (Zia)
♠ J 8 6
♡ J 10 6 5 2
◇ K 9 2
♣ Q 5

East (Jaggy)
♠ Q 9 2
♡ Q 9
◇ Q 10 4
♣ 9 8 7 3 2

South
♠ K 10 7 4
♡ A 7 3
◇ A 7 5
♣ A J 6

	Zia		Jaggy
South	West	North	East
1 NT	pass	3 NT	(all pass)

I led the ♡5 to Jaggy's queen. South won the second round with the ace, then cashed the ♠K. Jaggy played the 9!

South, who could no longer afford to duck my 8 on the next round, put up the ace, and Jaggy unblocked the queen.

Now I could win the third round of spades and clear the hearts.

South had eight tricks and, knowing that East had eight minor-suit cards to my five, misguessed the ♣Q — one down, and a big step forward in Pakistan-India relations.

Winning has its own satisfaction and, although no one except me seemed particularly impressed with the political magnitude of our achievement, I was sufficiently moved to write off the 200 francs.

Monte Carlo

After Cannes comes Monte Carlo. The mention of Monte Carlo conjures up images of the jet set: extravagance, elegance and beauty. For once, reality fits the image. The only thing small about Monte Carlo is its size — a mere two square kilometers, or about half the size of Central Park in New York.

The marriage of the beautiful Grace Kelly to her handsome prince gave the municipality a fairy-tale aura. The fascination of the world with royalty and glamor has done the rest. Wealth is still the key word, but banking, not gambling, is the principal industry. The rich move there not only to enjoy the playground but also for the more commercial reason that residents don't pay any taxes. Prices are astronomical, so be careful when you order a drink. The first time I was there, I offered someone a coke at Jimmy's, the famous nightclub, and it cost me £20.

However, no mention of Monte Carlo would be complete without an Omar story. Breaking the bank at Monte Carlo is every gambler's dream, but it's much more likely that the bank will break you. That doesn't always have to be as bad as it sounds — if you are a superstar like Omar Sharif. Omar once found himself at the losing end of a heavy night at the *chemin de fer* table. In fact, in bridge terminology, heavy was an underbid — he had lost everything he had, a small fortune.

Movie stars are not supposed to react to these setbacks like other mortals. So he started to leave the casino with as much dignity as his acting skills would permit. He had almost made it to the exit when a man stopped him. "Excuse me, Mr. Sharif, I am sorry about your loss." He spoke in Arabic.

"Thank you, but it was nothing. These things happen."

"I am a great fan of yours, and hope you will accept a tip from me that might help you recoup your losses. The price of silver is about to rise dramatically; buy some."

Omar took the advice, and the next day called a friend of his, Alan "Ace" Greenberg, President of Bear Stearns (an investment bank in New York), and also a keen bridge player. The tip was dynamite; a coup was in progress in the silver market, so Omar not only recovered his losses, but made a profit as well.

I visited Monte Carlo many times over the next few years, but sadly the annual tournament there has been discontinued, probably from a lack of sponsorship. The last time I was there, I was a spectator, not a player, in the 1976 World Championships. Every fourth year each country may send teams to compete in the Open and Women's Team events.

There are no money prizes, of course, but the competition is as fierce as it is in any other bridge event. A world championship gold medal is the most treasured prize for any duplicate player. Many teams featured players I knew well. I was jealous that they could represent their countries at this level. I too would have liked to be playing for my country, Pakistan, but that seemed no more than a hopeless dream.

6

Bridge is More Than
Just Holding Hands

Atlantic City, Monday Evening

During the first day's play, my emotions kept racing from the heights to the depths, keeping pace with the results I achieved. But toward the end of the session, I felt reasonably satisfied. Most of my partners had played well, and we had kept the number of errors to an acceptable minimum. I expected my score to be reasonable. It is an odd aspect of bridge that, unlike any other game or sport, you don't know your score until the end of the session. You have an approximate idea, but it isn't confirmed until some 15 minutes after play finishes, when the scores are posted.

Getting up from the table, I bumped into two old friends who were screaming at each other, and who looked on the verge of warfare. One of them, "Harry the Horse," was almost breathing fire as he snapped, snorted and screamed at his companion, Fred. Both are from New York and play regularly in the big money games there, but that is all they have in common. Harry, straight out of Guys and Dolls, is about 6' 6" and makes a living the hard way: betting on the horses. He is said to win over a million dollars a year doing this, but Harry never admits to anything where money is concerned. He certainly doesn't look like a million dollars — if you passed him in the street, you'd be more likely to offer him a dollar for a cup of soup than to ask him for a loan. As far as I can make out, Harry seems to possess only one shirt — I'd tell you the color but it is no longer possible to define it with any degree of exactness; and his favorite pair of checked trousers have long lost any pretence at fashion. Harry has his good points and his bad points. It is true that on occasion he doesn't smell too sweet, but to be fair he could tell you the finishing times and prices of all the Kentucky Derby winners for the past 10 years without even breathing hard. When he's not betting, Harry plays bridge. Harry loves bridge. He reads all the books, learns all the plays, knows all the conventions. Harry is a competent player, but he has one problem: He can't win; he doesn't even finish. Harry has won six-figure sums at the racetrack in an afternoon; in a bridge tournament he has placed several times, but nobody ever remembers him finishing in the winners' circle. There he's on a permanent losing streak.*

Fred, on the other hand, is a Taiwanese who settled in America. An engineer by trade, he came to this country as a student, got caught up in the American dream, and stayed. He works for a construction company by day and moonlights at bridge by night to support his ever-growing family. Fred is charming and well liked by everyone, but he becomes a cold and tough competitor when he sits at the bridge table. He wins consistently at money bridge but, like a lot of money players, is not too interested in tournaments and trophies. This tournament was the exception because of the high rewards. Without being technically much better than Harry,

---

*Just before this book went to press, Harry did win a U.S. National pair event! Congratulations, Harry. Savor it!

Fred does the right thing when it's needed — the mark of a winner.

Bridge quarrels and "fights" are inevitable. It doesn't make any difference how much you play. It is always easy for the result on a particular hand to drive one or both players over the edge. Rather like a duel, the argument continues until one party gets satisfaction — which usually entails his partner (the perpetrator) apologizing to him, or that a third party enter the picture, as in this particular fight. The Horse was getting nowhere, so he grabbed hold of me. Foaming at the mouth, he announced, "One of us needs a doctor, and it isn't me. Just tell this uneducated idiot that he doesn't understand the first thing about bidding, will you. You have this hand, sitting South:

♠ 9 4 ♡ A J 10 7 6 3 ◇ A Q 5 ♣ 6 2

"The bidding began:

	Fred		Harry
West	North	East	South
—	2 ♣*	pass	2 ♡
4 ◇*	6 ♣	pass	?

2 ♣ = strong, artificial and forcing
4 ◇ = preemptive, natural

"What would you have bid?"

This was tough. On the one hand, it looked as if I had a lot of tricks for partner; on the other hand, the unwritten law in these situations where one partner jumps to slam is that you should "leave him alone" unless you are absolutely certain he can make seven. It was a close decision, worthy of thought, but I was more interested in seeing the results of the afternoon's game than standing here any longer. I decided that Fred is a big boy, that the diamond holding looked dangerous, probably was opposite a void, and that if all my partner had needed was two aces, he could have used Blackwood. I said, "I pass."

Fred was beaming but Harry became more furious than before. He shouted, "You are useless, just as bad as he is. I bid the obvious seven clubs, and they doubled. Of course I converted to seven notrump in case they were ruffing something, and they doubled again. Then they cashed an ace. Would you believe it?"

C'est la vie, I thought. This was the layout:

North (Fred)
♠ K Q J 6
♡ K 4
◇ —
♣ A K Q J 10 9 8

West
♠ A 10 3
♡ 8
◇ K J 10 9 8 4 3
♣ 5 4

East
♠ 8 7 5 2
♡ Q 9 5 2
◇ 7 6 2
♣ 7 3

South (Harry the Horse)
♠ 9 4
♡ A J 10 7 6 3
◇ A Q 5
♣ 6 2

At the time I sympathized slightly with Harry, but later, on looking deeper, I changed my mind, deciding that seven clubs was an inferior bid. This is why:

1. Two hearts had already shown a positive with hearts.
2. We had been preempted — a signal for caution.
3. South had two aces; if that was all partner wanted, he

would have asked for them via Blackwood.

4. Partner took control of the auction; to overrule him required certainty, not conjecture.

Anyway, by now Harry had had his fill of both me and Fred. He stormed off, none too pleased.

Finally I was free to look at the results board. I expected to be well placed, but found that I wasn't even in the first 20 — I was lying 23rd. This was good enough to qualify, but not as comfortably placed as I would have liked or had thought I would be. I had been feeling pretty high, as is customary when you think you have done well, but now my mood changed totally. I was annoyed and frustrated. Then I remembered that I had a dinner appointment. I just had time for a shower and change before we were due to meet.

I was still feeling disappointed. Expectation is a double-edged and powerful emotion. In bridge it can be treacherous. On occasion it lifts you to great heights, only a moment later to flick you down again. If I had played badly and been out of luck, I would have felt relieved and happy at a standing of 23rd, with 40 to qualify. But having expected to be among the leaders, I was shattered by my disappointing position. The feeling is so similar to the emotional ups and downs of being in love. Both give you high expectations that can lead to despair or ecstasy. The pleasure of success is increased by comparison with the agony of failure. This is one of the reasons why bridge is so endlessly fascinating. No matter how much you play, or how proficient you become, you can never be in total control. While climbing out of the shower, I was appeased slightly by my own philosophizing. I accepted that there was nothing I could do about it; I would just have to play better tomorrow.

At least I had more chance than players in Pakistan had started with.

Pakistan, 1977

It wasn't bridge but politics that was responsible for my next move. Our business was going well, and my brother's thoughts once more reverted to politics. The government had changed in Pakistan, with the opposition party gaining power, and he became a senator. Family is family, so I returned home for a while to run the business while he concentrated on his political affairs. (However, I did commute to London regularly for rubber-bridge fixes.)

Throughout my years spent abroad, I had always looked forward to regular visits back home. Even though the number of days spent there have been few by comparison, I have always identified closely with my country of birth, and have always thought of it as home.

I may have been educated in the West, grown up with Western culture, and lived in countries of the West, but I feel that I am no more than a visitor. I love London, enjoy Paris, and find the excitement of New York thrilling, but it doesn't matter how long I've been away, whenever I head back to Pakistan I feel the reassuring comfort and security that only going home can bring.

I'm not sure why my loyalties are so strong. Perhaps it's connected to the nostalgia of seeing the house I knew as a child, the warmth of greeting family and friends. It might be no more than sentimentality, but maybe it's something deeper, an inseparable bond with a culture to which I belong yet hardly know.

Sometimes it's difficult to envisage how different the world can be, how cultures and customs vary from place to place as dramatically as the weather or the seasons — and how what is normal in one part of the world is an anathema in another.

Even if you are one of those people who occasionally reflects on such things, you would never think that such differences could apply to the game of bridge, but they do.

Bridge is a harmless pastime in most countries, but there are some nations where even today the word "bridge" is viewed suspiciously by the powers that be. There, either because of a lack of education or understanding of the game, it is viewed as an activity more closely related to gambling than to an intellectual contest. I should know, because Pakistan is one of those countries.

Ever since watching the 1976 World Championships in Monte Carlo, I had thought about the possibility of Pakistan participating internationally. *Even though I was theoretically eligible, it never occurred to me to consider representing any other country.* The problem was that I knew my hopes were unlikely to materialize because of the "anti" attitudes in my homeland. How do you represent a country in a sport that isn't a sport?

Until 1977 there wasn't even an official bridge club. Then one, just one, opened. It might not occur to you, as you visit your local bridge club, that you are doing something exciting, let alone dangerous. After all, what could be more mundane than a relaxed afternoon at the local club? "Mundane" would not be accurate to describe the atmosphere in our bridge club. In 1975, a bridge club was opened by a group of enthusiasts who wanted to hold a weekly duplicate game. The club lasted just one week! That's how long it took for the religious groups of the area to find out about it and have it closed.

In a way it was just as well; simply visiting the club was nerve-racking with the constant worry that at any time violent neighbors might turn up with their own brand of eviction notice.

We were ready to jump off the nearest balcony at the first sign of danger. The term "slip bid" took on a new dimension. . . .

After this mild attempt at organization, we slunk back to the privacy of our own houses for a while. But bridge players all over the world are a resilient lot, ours being more tenacious than most. Undaunted, we formed a Bridge Association, and even applied to the Government for recognition. This recognition was not immediately forthcoming, but meanwhile a compromise was reached. The good news was that we would be allowed to open a bridge club. The bad news was that it would have to be located in the changing room of the National Sports Stadium. The room was off the beaten track, dingy and tiny. But it was a start. Then a lucky break occurred. The Pakistan Bridge Association received an invitation to send a team to participate in the Far East Championships in Hong Kong.

Once more we faced government opposition, this time for reasons of international politics, because capitalist Taiwan was being represented. We would not be allowed to play against them, because of the objection from Mainland China. Another compromise; we had to give them a *walkover* whenever we were scheduled to play against them. Naturally that meant we had almost no chance of doing really well, but then again these were trying times. At least we were allowed to enter the competition — before you can win you must enter the race.

Forming a team, the next step, was easy. We simply invited anyone to show up who was prepared to pay his own expenses. We just managed to get six players. Reinforced with a few officials along for the ride, the Pakistan National Bridge Team had entered the world arena.

Not surprising, the opposition weren't particularly impressed by this team of newcomers, and for the most part disposed of us rather efficiently. The only bright spot was that in our first outing we did beat India, allowing us to save a little face on our return home. The rivalry between Pakistan and India is such that beating them is as important for us as winning a World Championship is for anyone else.

These excursions into the Far East became an annual event, and although not even the most generous would say that bridge in Pakistan was exactly booming, it was at least a start. It had the effect of stirring the martini of interest, if not shaking it too violently. Each year a few more people became available for selection. How much of this was due to the love of bridge and how much to the attraction of visiting one of the many exotic oriental countries, I'm not sure.

Most of our players are very emotional, but we quickly learned that team spirit and behavior were almost as important as how well we played. We devised our own set of rules. Apologizing for an error can be very difficult, so we even incorporated an "I'm-sorry-partner" bid into our system:

West	North	East	South
—	1 NT	pass	2 ♠*
pass	2 NT	pass	3 ♠

2 ♠ = a transfer to two notrump
3 ♠ = a transfer to three notrump with the message: "Sorry about that previous hand, partner."

Three spades had no other meaning in our methods. The opener had no idea what the responder held, but it worked and never failed to raise a smile.

Our next task was to form partnerships and a regular team. This was harder than it sounds because our few good players were spread all over the world. I was lucky to find a partner, Masood Salim, whose composure was well suited to my more exuberant style. At that time his English was limited. He had never read a bridge book, but his natural talent was enormous. We are still going strong some 15 years later.

Masood is one of the few partners with whom I feel confident when laying down my dummy. In one of our excursions, he showed his flair when he made a four-spade contract by completely fooling the player in the West position (see the following deal). He did this by making a rare double-duck, which demonstrates the importance of imagination in bridge.

East dealer
All vulnerable

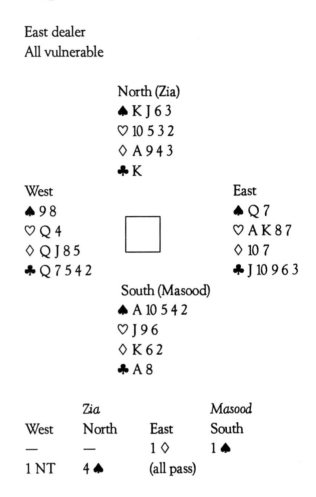

North (Zia)
♠ K J 6 3
♡ 10 5 3 2
♢ A 9 4 3
♣ K

West
♠ 9 8
♡ Q 4
♢ Q J 8 5
♣ Q 7 5 4 2

East
♠ Q 7
♡ A K 8 7
♢ 10 7
♣ J 10 9 6 3

South (Masood)
♠ A 10 5 4 2
♡ J 9 6
♢ K 6 2
♣ A 8

	Zia		Masood
West	North	East	South
—	—	1 ◊	1 ♠
1 NT	4 ♠	(all pass)	

The bidding requires some explanation. The New Zealand pair sitting East-West were playing a high-tech system of relays and computer-like sequences. East's opening bid of one diamond was artificial. It meant he had 10-15 points and no five-card major. He couldn't open one club because, in this system, that would have been strong, showing 16-plus points. Then, after Masood, South, made the normal one-spade overcall, West bid an "unusual" one notrump, which meant he had the minors. Sitting North, I decided to end all this nonsense by leaping to game.

West led the ◊ Q, and Masood studied the hand before playing to the opening lead, a practice that average players would do well to copy. With four obvious red-suit losers, Massood's only chance seemed to be to pitch one of his hearts on dummy's fourth diamond. But this would require losing a diamond trick, thus giving the opponents the chance to cash their three heart tricks.

Rather than expose the situation, Masood ducked in both hands, pretending that he didn't hold the ◊ K.

Pity poor West, who had to find a heart shift to defeat the contract. Instead, he continued diamonds at trick two. Noting the fall of East's 10, Masood thanked him silently, winning with the king. He then drew two rounds of trumps and led a diamond from his hand, finessing dummy's 9. On the ◊ A, Masood discarded a losing heart.

This beautiful double-duck not only succeeded in fulfilling the contract, but it also put a psychological damper on our opponents' outlook for the rest of the match. Players do not like it when an opponent makes a game that could have been defeated. They like it even less when they are fooled in the process — which is one reason I enjoy playing with Masood: If I am his partner, he can never do it to me!

The pot of gold waiting for the winner of the Zonal Tournament was the opportunity to play in the World Championships for the Bermuda Bowl, easily the most coveted prize in bridge. Every two years the winners of the various zonal tournaments around the world would meet at the playoffs — something like the Davis Cup in tennis.

Such lofty ambitions were still not in our sights, although our standings did improve with experience. If only we weren't restricted by our walkover loss to Taiwan — but that would take a miracle.

Calcutta

Meanwhile, friendly competition with India *was* on the menu. If you leave behind the rhetoric of the politicians, the people of India and Pakistan are really very close. We are two countries but one people. Thousands of families have members in both countries, and memories of days gone by are still very much alive, especially in the hearts of the older generation. Each year we would look forward to attending the December Bridge Congress in Calcutta.

Calcutta is without a doubt amongst the dirtiest and dustiest cities in the world. The population is so huge that, at almost any time of the day or night, the crowds on the pavements outnumber in density a combined concert of Madonna and the Rolling Stones. Yet, Calcutta is also the most special city in the world — for its people. A voyager could travel the world without encountering anything comparable to Calcutta's overwhelming warmth and hospitality. And this is in a country already famous for its kindness to visitors. Tourists traverse the world to see its various wonders. This is Calcutta's wonder and, in itself, sufficient reason to visit the city.

The actual play was held at the Saturday Club, where the picturesque green lawns still echo with the ghosts of the British Raj. There were literally hundreds of kibitzers (spectators) crowding around our table at the start of play in the pairs. The sheer numbers of these enthusiasts forced the organizers to move our table from the playing hall into the spacious gardens behind. Although this slightly inconvenienced the East-West pairs who had to make the detour, it was, in practice, the only way to accommodate the throng.

I remember this hand:

East dealer
North-South vulnerable

North
♠ A 9 2
♡ Q J 4
◇ A 7 3 2
♣ A 10 5

West
♠ K 10 5 4
♡ 9 8 7 6
◇ J 6
♣ 8 6 3

East
♠ 8 7 6 3
♡ 10 2
◇ 10 9 8 4
♣ K 7 2

South (Roy)
♠ Q J
♡ A K 5 3
◇ K Q 5
♣ Q J 9 4

West	North	East	Roy South
—	—	pass	1 NT
pass	4 NT	pass	6 NT
(all pass)			

Officially the one-notrump opening by Debashis Roy showed 15-17 points, but he not unreasonably devalued the ♠Q-J doubleton and counted his 18 points as 17.

The opening lead was the ♡9. Assuming the ♣K was badly placed, South saw that he needed a diamond break, or a winning spade finesse, or a squeeze (if one defender held the ♠K and four diamonds). But if the diamonds were not breaking, should he play for the spade finesse or the squeeze?

Roy had an ace up his sleeve (or should I say a jack?). He was determined to use the fact that he was a point heavy for

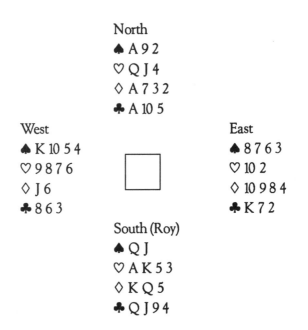

North
♠ A 9 2
♡ Q J 4
◊ A 7 3 2
♣ A 10 5

West
♠ K 10 5 4
♡ 9 8 7 6
◊ J 6
♣ 8 6 3

East
♠ 8 7 6 3
♡ 10 2
◊ 10 9 8 4
♣ K 7 2

South (Roy)
♠ Q J
♡ A K 5 3
◊ K Q 5
♣ Q J 9 4

his opening bid. Roy won the opening heart lead in hand and finessed the ♣Q, losing to the king. He won the heart return in the dummy, cashed the ♡J and ♣A, then returned to hand with the ◊Q. He played off his fourth heart and the ♣J.

At this point, West had seen 15 points in declarer's hand. So when Roy led the ♠Q, can you blame West for covering, "knowing" that South couldn't have the jack? Roy was able to claim.

If the ♠Q hadn't been covered, Roy would have taken the inference that West didn't have the king. He would have put up dummy's ♠A and played for a squeeze against East. Neat!

Two incidents stand out.

While playing in Calcutta I met an unforgettable bridge player, a young man called Om Parkash Chaudry. He is memorable not for his standard of play, which was high enough, but because he was blind. Moreover, he played without the benefit of Braille cards. A friend would sit behind him, whispering to him just once what his cards were as he picked them up. Similarly, if Om became the declarer, his friend would name dummy's cards as well. Om would call his cards whenever it was his turn to play either on defense or as declarer. He rarely made a mistake, and would do this hand after hand, playing not only well but at normal speed.

The first time I saw him, I was impressed and asked him to play in a tournament with me. He agreed, and we played a few days later in a pair event. We were doing well enough and Om was in the middle of playing a hand, when the electricity failed, a not uncommon occurrence in India.

The play around him stopped, but Om, oblivious to what was happening, continued calling for a card from the dummy.

"You'll have to wait, the lights have gone out," I informed him. Before I realized the significance of my own remark, Om answered, "I'm sorry, I forgot that you can't play bridge with the lights out." Just an innocent statement, but a lesson at the same time, equally valuable in life and bridge. Try to understand a situation from the other person's point of view. Things often look very different from the other side.

The second incident was more humorous. When I started to play bridge seriously, I remember people asking me, "Just how far can bridge take you?" It was in Calcutta that I might have found the answer to that question. It started with an opening lead problem, one that literally took our team from Calcutta to Delhi.

You hold as West:

♠ 8 3 ♡ 8 7 5 ◇ K 7 6 3 ♣ K 8 7 5

The bidding goes as follows:

You

West	North	East	South
—	1 ♣*	pass	2 ♣*
pass	2 ♡	pass	2 ♠
pass	3 ♠	pass	4 ♣
pass	4 ♡	pass	4 ♠
pass	4 NT*	pass	5 ◇*
pass	6 ♠	pass	pass
pass			

1 ♣ = Precision: at least 16 points.
2 ♣ = eight-plus points and at least five clubs
4 NT = Roman Keycard Blackwood
5 ◇ = one keycard, counting the four aces and the
        king of spades as keycards

What would you lead?

At the time I had a penchant for leading honors whenever
possible, probably because I thought it looked good. It is not
usual practice, so a player who succeeds in this play stands
out. But here it also happened to be technically correct. The
king of diamonds *was* the only lead to defeat the contract.
The full deal looked like this:

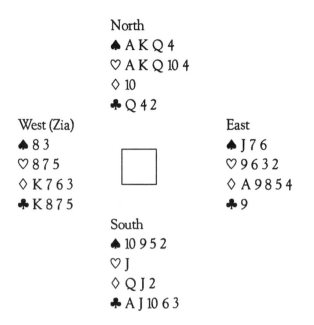

North
♠ A K Q 4
♡ A K Q 10 4
◊ 10
♣ Q 4 2

West (Zia)
♠ 8 3
♡ 8 7 5
◊ K 7 6 3
♣ K 8 7 5

East
♠ J 7 6
♡ 9 6 3 2
◊ A 9 8 5 4
♣ 9

South
♠ 10 9 5 2
♡ J
◊ Q J 2
♣ A J 10 6 3

On a low diamond lead, declarer is able to take a ruffing finesse on the second round to establish a 12th trick (five trump tricks, five hearts, one diamond and one club trick).

The good thing about a play like the ◊K opening lead is that if it fails, it is hidden away, whereas if it works, it gets great press. This was the case here, but the story didn't end there. A few days later our team had to fly to Delhi. We arrived at Calcutta Airport to find that a bureaucratic slip-up had resulted in our not having the required visas. Travel through India is restricted for Pakistanis, and so we were told that we would have to wait two or three days. A situation that could have turned out to be rather annoying was saved by my lead in Calcutta. When we discovered that one of the senior officials was a bridge fanatic who had been following the results at the tournament, we appealed to him. Ignoring the usual red tape, he granted permission on condition that I answered just one question: "How on earth did you lead the king of diamonds?"

This is what I explained: "The way to tackle a lead

problem is to analyze the bidding. What do we know? North has at least five hearts and four spades, while South has four spades and at least five clubs. There must be a key card missing, otherwise North would have tried for seven. North has no more than four minor-suit cards. His use of Blackwood means that he has a diamond control and my king of diamonds confirms that it is the ace or a singleton. It must be right to attack diamonds before any losers in that suit can be pitched on the good hearts.

"Can it make any difference which diamond to lead? Yes. If North has a singleton and South has a dangerous holding like ◊ A-J-10 or ◊ Q-J-4, leading a low diamond to partner's queen or ace would allow declarer to make an extra trick later by taking a ruffing finesse. If you're going to play partner for a diamond honor, it can hardly cost to start with the king."

The explanation had the desired effect. If the game would take me no further, it had at least taken us from Calcutta to Delhi.

The story of our international bridge career would probably have ended there if fate hadn't seen fit to play a hand. The World Bridge Federation decided to increase the number of zones. Pakistan would now fall under a new zone known as "Asia and the Middle East." Our guardian angel had worked the miracle we needed. Not only would we no longer have to forfeit to Taiwan, but also the new group would be much weaker than the previous one. We would in effect just have to beat India to qualify for the Bermuda Bowl. No more walkovers!

And that came to pass soon after at the championships in Bangalore, India. We narrowly beat the Indian team and qualified to play in Rye, New York, in the 1981 Bermuda Bowl.

7

Pros and Cons

Atlantic City, Monday Evening: Dinner

I arrived at the lobby to find that our dinner group had swelled slightly; from our original three — Tim, the Weasel and myself — we had become eight. All were welcome contributors to the standard dinner conversation at all bridge tournaments: the postmortem of hands.

If you walk into a normal Chinese restaurant, you expect to hear the click of mishandled chop-sticks and familiar references to Shark's Fin Soup and Peking Duck. If you see the diners staring at pieces of paper, the odds are that they are reading about their fortunes from the fortune cookies.

If you silently agree with the above scenario, I can bet you've never eaten in a Chinese restaurant when there's a bridge tournament in the area. Now the mouths full of Chow Mein sputter out indignant protests as to why their partners led back a heart instead of a spade. The more genteel occupants gulp down huge swallows of Chinese beer to leave their mouths free to dissect some intricate bidding sequence, while others, hands still wet with hoisin sauce leaking from the duck pancakes, grab hold of pieces of paper that don't contain their horoscopes but are hand records of the session they have just finished.

The usual practice is to take a few minutes ordering the dinner, then spend a few hours going over every hand played during the day. The diners usually try hard to linger over the hands where they shone, and to stuff their mouths with Szechuan chicken or other delicacies when their less distinguished moments are about to be spotlighted.

These postmortems are great, but not only for the fun of reminiscing. They can actually be of enormous benefit to any standard player, an opportunity to learn and improve. And there is no limit to improvement. An expert can learn something from a beginner, as much as from another expert. There's nothing demeaning in this fact. In bridge, *ego* is sometimes useful, but *hubris* is too dangerous a luxury. If a player listens to the views of others at these sessions, if he carefully registers and records his errors, listing them under category and type, he will improve.

I know several members of the once famous but now defunct Aces team, which was formed by Ira J. Corn, Jr., a Texas oil-baron, to recover the World Championship from the Italians. After every match, they used their postmortems as self-teaching forums. They had a system of marking their errors. They would put each mistake into one of seven brackets, their Seven Deadly Sins:

1. No-win declarer-play: dumb dummy-play.
2. No-win defense: indefensible strategy.
3. Unilateral bidding: solo flights of fancy.
4. Overbidding: freefall parachute jumping without a ripcord.
5. Technical errors: the computer blew a fuse.

6. System violation: the amnesia syndrome.
7. Impulsive bidding: the matador without a cape.

I think it is useful to keep a record of your errors. You will soon discover your individual strengths and weaknesses, which probably will be concentrated in specific areas. Each person is different. Maybe your slam bidding lets you down; or your opening leads; or your competitive bidding — even all three. You can only cure something you have diagnosed, which is why I am stressing this point. What was good enough for the Aces is good enough for the world. Anything that gets you to analyze your results cannot help but be beneficial.

* * * * * * * * *

Meanwhile, back at the restaurant, someone asked the Weasel what the Tournament Director was doing at his table in the afternoon. The Weasel was already breaking doctor's orders by eating a spicy beef dish when he was meant to be on a diet. But at the time I thought he may not live to have a heart attack because it was probable that he would burst a blood vessel before he finished the story he was excitedly telling us.

"Who says these players are experts?" he screamed. "They're fools, they're beginners. Even my daughter could play better." The Weasel had the attention of the table.

"I am playing with a lady whom I've never seen before, and hope I'll never see again. I've been nice to her and agreed to play all the conventions she wants, even though most of them aren't fit for discussion, let alone playing. In return for playing her way, I tell her that all I want her to do is to try not to revoke and to follow my signals. If I play a high card, she should continue; if I play low, she should switch. Isn't that really simple?"

Immediately I thought that if it had been "really simple" to the lady in question, we wouldn't have been hearing this. But like the others, I nodded agreement, eager to hear the end of the tale.

"We end up defending four hearts. *She* leads the king of spades. I play the two, hoping for a club switch. *She* continues with another spade. Declarer plays a diamond, which *she* wins with the ace. I play the two, begging for a club switch, but *she* continues a diamond. When she got in yet again with a trump, she still wouldn't play a club, allowing declarer to make this impossible contract."

The Weasel was turning a strange shade of purple. Worried about his blood pressure, I made him take a drink of water to calm down. Someone else took over the story.

"Suddenly everyone started yelling for the police, claiming the Weasel had gone berserk. He had torn his cards into pieces and thrown them away. The director asked him if it was true that he had torn up his cards, and if he had anything to say in his defense.

"The Weasel tried to look innocent. 'Oh, no,' he replied, 'I dropped them on the floor and they broke.' "

At this everybody broke into peals of laughter, and even the Weasel recovered enough to grin.

Upon returning to the hotel I saw Paul Chemla, the French player, walking sadly around the casino floor, muttering unintelligible French words to himself. When I asked him why he was following this odd pattern, he announced with his usual exaggeration that he wished he had never come to America and was seriously contemplating suicide.

"Everybody kills me all day. First as partners they don't know how to take a finesse, and then as opponents they misbid and end up in ridiculous contracts, which they make thanks to miraculous lies of the cards. To make matters worse, the food is horrible, and the croupiers at the blackjack table hate me and take all my money. What else is there for me to do except commit suicide?"

Chemla is a very bright guy, and a disciplined and controlled bridge player. Yet somehow, like many other disciplined people in and out of the bridge world, he can't resist an undisciplined flutter at the tables. His gambling losses are legendary. In fact he flutters with his money until he has nothing left to flutter. I find it amazing the way gambling can totally influence, even change, a person's character. I admit to being undisciplined in the casino, but at least I am consistent and play bridge the same way.

It's a sort of Jekyll & Hyde syndrome that is difficult to explain. Changing the subject, I asked him about the French team for the World Championships. France and Brazil are the only bridge nations that have any claim to challenging the supremacy of the Americans at the international level. France has eight to ten of the very best players, but rivalries and differences mean that they rarely play together. The Americans have 80 to 100, and therefore have less difficulty in putting together a good team. Most other nations have no more than two world-class players.

Chemla normally changes his partners like other people their ties, but his present confrère, Michel Perron, is top class and unflappable, which is crucial for playing with Chemla. Earlier in his career, Chemla had partnered Michel Lebel, who is more temperamental, though a great player. I remember a board, in different rooms, on which both Chemla and Lebel played brilliantly. It came up during the Rosenblum Teams at the Miami Olympiad in 1986.

South dealer
None vulnerable

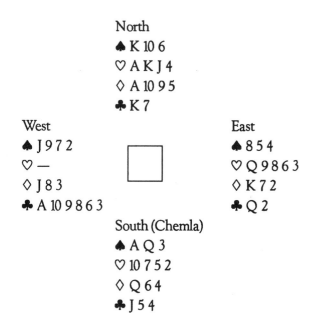

North
♠ K 10 6
♡ A K J 4
◇ A 10 9 5
♣ K 7

West
♠ J 9 7 2
♡ —
◇ J 8 3
♣ A 10 9 8 6 3

East
♠ 8 5 4
♡ Q 9 8 6 3
◇ K 7 2
♣ Q 2

South (Chemla)
♠ A Q 3
♡ 10 7 5 2
◇ Q 6 4
♣ J 5 4

In Miami there was a VuGraph presentation. The action at one table was displayed on a large screen, while the bids and plays of the other table were relayed from the closed room on to the same screen. Commentators analyzed the deal as play progressed.

Chemla

South	West	North	East
pass	pass	1 ◇	pass
1 ♡	pass	3 NT*	pass
4 ♡	(all pass)		

3 NT = a balanced raise to four hearts.

With the trumps breaking 5-0 offside, four hearts looked nearly impossible. But Chemla made the contract in about 40 seconds! He won the low spade lead in the dummy with the king, then cashed the ♡A, getting the bad news. Chemla took his two spade winners before leading a diamond to the 10 and king. East returned a diamond, declarer winning in hand with the queen. Chemla led a club to the king (West ducked his ace), cashed the ◊A, and led the last diamond, ruffed by East and overruffed by South. That left this position:

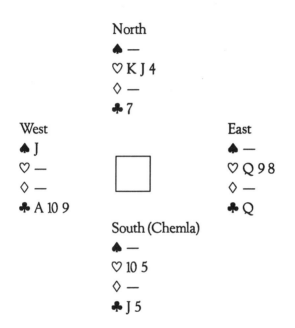

North
♠ —
♡ K J 4
◊ —
♣ 7

West
♠ J
♡ —
◊ —
♣ A 10 9

East
♠ —
♡ Q 9 8
◊ —
♣ Q

South (Chemla)
♠ —
♡ 10 5
◊ —
♣ J 5

Chemla exited with a club, which West won with the ace in order to lead another club. East was able to overruff the dummy, but then had to lead from his ♡Q-9 into dummy's ♡K-J. Plus 420.

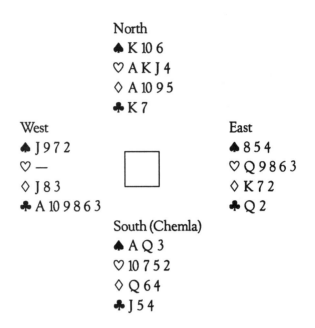

North
- ♠ K 10 6
- ♡ A K J 4
- ◇ A 10 9 5
- ♣ K 7

West
- ♠ J 9 7 2
- ♡ —
- ◇ J 8 3
- ♣ A 10 9 8 6 3

East
- ♠ 8 5 4
- ♡ Q 9 8 6 3
- ◇ K 7 2
- ♣ Q 2

South (Chemla)
- ♠ A Q 3
- ♡ 10 7 5 2
- ◇ Q 6 4
- ♣ J 5 4

In the Closed Room, this was the auction:

			Lebel
South	West	North	East
pass	pass	1 ♣*	1 ♡
double*	2 ♣	3 ♣*	pass
3 NT	(all pass)		

1 ♣ = Precision: 16-plus points
double = negative
3 ♣ = asking for a club stopper for notrump

Defending against three notrump, West led the ♣10. We are all told to play third hand high. As a general rule, this is a good one; but it takes a great player to find the right time to break the rule. Here, Lebel was East. When dummy played low, so did he! Declarer could have made the contract by ducking, but naturally he won with the jack. When a heart finesse lost to East, Lebel returned the ♣Q. His partner overtook with the ace and cashed four more club tricks.

Here is another example of the same principle when defending against a notrump contract:

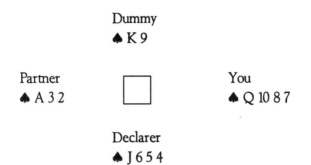

Dummy
♠ K 9

Partner
♠ A 3 2

You
♠ Q 10 8 7

Declarer
♠ J 6 5 4

Suppose you know from the bidding that declarer has four spades. When partner leads the deuce and declarer plays the 9, if you play the 10, you get three tricks when partner gains the lead.

Chemla, who wasn't in the mood to discuss bridge hands, headed back toward the blackjack table. I decided to have an early night and carefully avoided the usual group of experts still carrying out postmortems. This was not so much to be fresh for the bridge tomorrow, but because we had a foursome of golf scheduled at the ridiculously early hour of 8:30 a.m.

London, The "Pros"

In most sports, like golf, football or tennis, being a professional is an achievement, signifying that the person is good enough to make a living from his skills. Professionals earn respect and fortunes in their chosen fields.

For some reason, bridge is a different story. I doubt there are any professional bridge players in Britain — meaning players who actually live off the game. For a reason I still haven't understood, in a bridge club the biggest insult you can pay someone is to call him a professional. It is a word used scathingly to describe a player who wins regularly.

This is somewhat ironic as I've never met anyone who played to lose. It's true that you don't need to play bridge for money to enjoy the game, but if you do play for a stake, then naturally you want to win. True, some players expect to lose and don't mind doing so too much. But surely everyone prefers the pleasure of winning, and, in my experience, the more you win, the greater the pleasure. Anyone who denies this is probably fooling himself.

In North America, however, there are true bridge professionals. They don't risk their own money at the rubber-bridge table; instead, they compete on the tournament circuit. They are paid fees by their partners, clients who want to learn more about the game or who wish to win. The top pros earn a good living in this way.

Why are the Americans by far the best players in the world today? This "play for pay" is one reason. The top Americans can afford to devote themselves full-time to bridge, and in any sport it is nearly always impossible for amateurs to compete successfully against professionals.

Watching the good players taught me a lot, with perhaps the best lesson being that the biggest winners weren't always the best technical players. Rubber bridge isn't a game; it's a way of life. It is most important to have the mentality of a winner.

Having said that, only a special kind of person can win regularly — unless, of course, he plays only with technically far inferior players. To beat your equals or near-equals requires a special sort of thinking, one that I needed to master. I started observing the experts whom I had encountered, and there were many to learn from.

To give you some examples, first there was Terence Reese, arguably the best player ever, and without doubt the best writer. There is a story that his concentration level is so fierce that he did not notice a naked woman walking around his table while he was playing a difficult contract.

With firm views on every subject, a dry, sarcastic humor that is very British, and a brilliant mind, Reese is excellent company. Sadly, by the time I was playing rubber bridge regularly in London, his interest in the game was waning, and to ascertain his opinion on a bidding problem usually required slipping him the question on a piece of paper while he was playing backgammon. His strengths were his logical mind and faultless technique, but he was also a practical player, who comfortably dealt with reality when required.

In his book, Reese on Play, Terence, playing South, needed to locate a missing queen in this hand:

South declarer
All vulnerable

North
♠ A 6 4
♡ A 7 5
◇ Q J 9 5 3
♣ 4 3

South
♠ K Q J
♡ K J 10
◇ K 10 6 4
♣ A K 7

South	West	North	East
2 NT	pass	3 ◇	pass
3 NT*	pass	6 NT	(all pass)

3 NT = With a minimum and only one ace, he didn't
show any enthusiasm for diamonds.

Reese won the club lead, drove out the ◇A, and won the
club return. Now he had to find the ♡Q to make his contract.

He tried a "dry run." First he led the ♠J from his hand. His
left-hand opponent fidgeted slightly — obviously trying to
mislead Reese into thinking he had the queen — and then
played low. Reese won with dummy's ♠A, and returned to
hand with a diamond.

Now, aware of his opponent's habits, he attacked the heart
suit, leading the ♡J. This time Reese's left-hand opponent
played low smoothly, so Reese finessed — successfully.

We've all been in games where a player hesitates with a
singleton or pretends to have a problem when he doesn't.

This sort of behavior is actually a mild form of cheating. In a tournament you can call the director, but in a more casual game at home, the culprit is often allowed to get away with it.

Maybe one day they'll know better, but meanwhile you should take advantage. The next time you've cut out of a rubber, don't wander away but watch the game. Focus closely not just on the bidding and play, but the *manner* in which people bid and play their cards. If they are going to play poker on the bridge table, find out their style and use it against them.

However, remember two things: first, you mustn't look at even the backs of the opponents cards when you're playing. Second, you must never take advantage of your partner's hesitations, but you may take advantage of your opponents' hesitations — though you do it at your own risk.

Boris Shapiro, Reese's ex-partner, is volatile and opinionated, but very colorful and never boring. Today he is a young man in his 80s, still playing bridge regularly. He finished an amazing second in the 1991 Sunday Times Invitation Pairs Tournament, an event of the very highest standard. He had the habit of playing with his poodle, Vodka, resting on his lap, but, as his partners will tell you, his bidding was very un-poodle-like. From Boris I learned that bridge is also a game played with heart and feeling.

Jeremy Flint, who died in November 1989, was at the top of British bridge for almost 30 years. He was a qualified lawyer, and on occasion used his training to think his way out of difficult situations.

He once held this hand:

♠ — ♡ 2 ◇ A K Q J 10 9 7 6 4 3 ♣ K 2

He was partnered with a notorious overbidder, who
opened four spades, which traditionally could show any sort
of garbage with a seven- or eight-card suit.

Flint naturally wanted to play in five diamonds, but
bidding a minor at the five-level would be taken as a cuebid
agreeing spades. That was out, but Blackwood was a possibility. If his partner responded five diamonds to four notrump,
he could pass. However, there was too great a chance that
the response would be five clubs and the situation would
worsen. Flint found an ingenious solution. Can you work out
how he solved his problem?

Improvisation is often necessary, so while you are thinking
about that, here's another one on a similar theme.

You're nonvulnerable against vulnerable opponents. Your
partner opens one heart, and you're holding this sorry collection:

♠ 8 2 ♡ K 7 6 3 ◇ 7 5 2 ♣ 9 8 3 2

It is true that if you judged to pass at this point, you would
escape criticism. But you've had a few glasses of Château
Lafite '45 at dinner, and you are playing against your least
favorite opponents. Still slightly tipsy, you mischievously
psych a one-spade response! OK? OK. Partner takes you
seriously and raises to three spades. How can you try to
extricate yourself from this rather embarrassing turn of
events?

Here are the "answers," but remember they're not 100
percent guaranteed to work.

On the first hand, with the 10 solid diamonds, Flint cuebid
five clubs! Partner was bound to have a singleton or void in

diamonds. As expected, his partner cuebid five diamonds. Flint cooly passed. Now you can follow the logic — or lack of it.

On the second hand, cuebid four diamonds (holding your breath and uttering a silent prayer). Partner will often save you with a cuebid of four hearts.

There were also the rebels. There are countless stories about the legendary John Collings, perhaps the greatest "flair" (or natural) player of all time.*

He was also one of the greatest overbidders. I remember that, in particular in fourth seat, he would open three notrump with any kind of hand, balanced or unbalanced, weak or strong. You never had an idea what he held, and — most annoying of all — he had a habit of making the contract!

I'm sure if I told you that once he bid and made seven hearts missing the K-Q-10-7-5 of hearts, you wouldn't believe me. But it is true. Here's how it happened:

---

*The technical player always looks for the right percentage play, basically ignoring the vibes at the table. A natural player is far more interested in using his table presence. Sometimes he will apparently play against the odds when he is sure it is right to do so. In my opinion, a natural player will normally be a bigger winner than a technician.

South dealer
North-South vulnerable

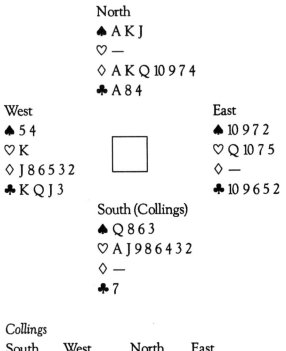

North
♠ A K J
♡ —
◊ A K Q 10 9 7 4
♣ A 8 4

West
♠ 5 4
♡ K
◊ J 8 6 5 3 2
♣ K Q J 3

East
♠ 10 9 7 2
♡ Q 10 7 5
◊ —
♣ 10 9 6 5 2

South (Collings)
♠ Q 8 6 3
♡ A J 9 8 6 4 3 2
◊ —
♣ 7

Collings

South	West	North	East
pass	pass	2 ♣	pass
2 ♡	pass	4 NT	pass
5 ◊	pass	7 ◊	pass
pass	double	pass	pass
7 ♡	double	(all pass)	

Collings trusted his partner the first time when he passed seven diamonds. But when West doubled, he retreated to his own eight-card heart suit.

Against this "impossible" grand slam, West led the ♣K. Collings won with dummy's ace, then led the ◊A. East ruffed with the ♡5, so Collings overruffed with the ♡6. Over to dummy with a spade to the king, Collings called for the ◊K, East ruffing with the ♡7 and he overruffed with the ♡8.

Back to dummy with another spade, Collings led the ♢Q. Once more, East ruffed low, this time with the ♡10. Collings overruffed with the ♡J, then cashed the ♡A, collecting the ♡K and ♡Q.

"We were lucky the trumps split," quipped Collings.

His operations were not always successful. Collings had a penchant for passing distributional hands, entering the bidding later at the four or five level. Once he passed this hand:

♠ A K Q J 10 7 6 4 3 2 ♡ 5 ♢ 7 ♣ 4

The bidding continued pass-pass-pass! Collings asked his partner what he held. The reply was, "Just three bare aces."

Then there is the lovable, if roguish, Scot, Irving Rose. He made his bids in Cockney rhyming slang, as unintelligible to me now as then. Two of the expressions he used were "monkey" and "carpet" (500 and 800, respectively), terms borrowed from horse-racing.

He is another flair player with a great nose for what is happening at the table. I remember the time I saw him pick up this hand:

♠ 4 ♡ 9 8 2 ♢ K Q J 10 8 7 5 4 ♣ 2

Nonvulnerable against vulnerable, his partner opened three clubs, promising, under their agreement, two of the top three honors. The next player overcalled four spades. What would you bid now?

Rose jumped to six clubs! He was planning, of course, to run to six diamonds if doubled. But the next player, sure that his partner was short in clubs, took the bait and bid six spades.

This came back to Rose, and he added insult to injury by

doubling. He was taking the 2-to-1 chance that his partner had the ♣A. Rose led his singleton club, partner did win with the ace and did return the suit for Rose to ruff. With apologies to Cyrano de Bergerac, that's what I call a nose!

He hasn't lost his touch. As recently as 1990, in the Netherlands, Rose held this hand:

♠ 4 ♡ 9 ♢ A Q J 7 6 ♣ K J 10 8 4 3

His partner bid one spade, his right-hand opponent over-called four hearts, and he was faced with a problem of how to find the right minor (a bid of four notrump would be Blackwood).

For him, the solution was simple — what else but bid four spades! He was sure the opponents would double, and then he could bid four notrump — this time unusual — and find the better minor-suit fit.

His plan backfired when four spades was passed out! But his genius was not lacking because four spades made!

This type of play was the kind I found the most exciting (and still do). I revelled in pulling off a "coup" against the opponents, often ignoring the many losses I incurred to get there. It was always the lure of that one beautiful moment that lay waiting in the wings.

Martin Hoffman is another memorable player. He is one of the best card players I have ever seen. He has to be, to make up for his eternal losing streak on the dogs and horses. He has had an amazing life, having been rescued from Auschwitz at the age of eight and brought to England. Without any formal education, he took up bridge, and is another natural. Hoffman plays more quickly than anyone else I have seen. His only drawback is that his bidding is very optimistic. I remember this conversation after a matchpoint event:

"Martin, what was your score on board 35?"

"Minus fifty," came Hoffman's reply.

"Yes, everyone seems to have gone down in four spades. Couldn't it be made?"

"Four spades? Oh no, I went one down in *six* spades. I couldn't make *that!*"

That was his way: playing a contract two levels higher than everyone else but taking two more tricks, for an average.

Hoffman is a master of inducing errors from his opponents. Suppose you are looking at this everyday holding:

Dummy

♠ 9 8 2

☐

Declarer

♠ A K 7 6 5

How do you play the suit to make as many tricks as possible?

Most players would incorrectly start with the ace. Perhaps they would cash the ace and king, hoping for a 3-2 break. But you would do better to lead the ♠9 from dummy. No matter how sweet-natured you are, if you're a bridge player, you love making the opponents look foolish. This might be the layout:

Dummy
♠ 9 8 2

West
♠ Q

East
♠ J 10 4 3

Declarer
♠ A K 7 6 5

East might be tempted to cover with the ♠10, whereupon you will lose no tricks, later finessing East out of his jack. The principle is always to start by leading the highest card possible from the short hand, tempting a cover.

Of course, if East plays low, you put up the ace. When the queen appears, it is correct to continue with a low spade to the ♠8, preparing for a finesse against East's remaining honor if the suit breaks 4-1.

Similarly:

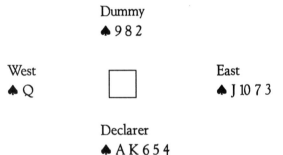

Dummy
♠ 9 8 2

West
♠ Q

East
♠ J 10 7 3

Declarer
♠ A K 6 5 4

If you lead the ♠9 from the dummy and East covers with the ♠10, you will lose only one trick instead of two.

How about the thrill you will feel if you make a small slam missing the ace, king and 10 of trumps. Impossible, you say? Maybe, maybe not.

Let's look at this deal:

North
♠ Q 8 5 4 3
♡ A Q 5
◇ K 7
♣ A 6 4

West
♠ A
♡ 8 7 3
◇ Q J 10 8 3
♣ J 9 8 3

East (The Teacher)
♠ K 10
♡ J 10 6 4 2
◇ 9 6 4 2
♣ 10 5

South (You)
♠ J 9 7 6 2
♡ K 9
◇ A 5
♣ K Q 7 2

You

South	West	North	East
1 ♠	pass	4 NT	pass
5 ◇	pass	6 ♠	(all pass)

You opened the bidding with one spade — "clearly" a mistake, because partner wouldn't stop bidding. Worse, East is "The Teacher" — you'll never hear the end of it.

You're in six spades, so you might as well try to make it. Naturally, after winning the ◇ Q lead in the dummy, leading a low spade won't help. Your best chance is to call for the ♠ Q. Maybe East will cover with the king, maybe even the teacher.

Similarly:

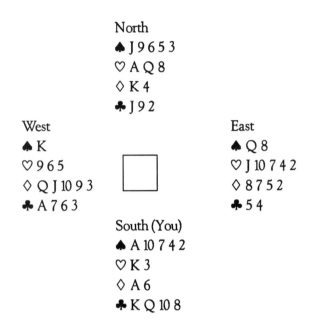

North
♠ J 9 6 5 3
♡ A Q 8
♢ K 4
♣ J 9 2

West
♠ K
♡ 9 6 5
♢ Q J 10 9 3
♣ A 7 6 3

East
♠ Q 8
♡ J 10 7 4 2
♢ 8 7 5 2
♣ 5 4

South (You)
♠ A 10 7 4 2
♡ K 3
♢ A 6
♣ K Q 10 8

Again, you are in six spades, this time with a definite loser in clubs and a possible trump loser. Lead the ♠J from the dummy. A friendly East will cover with the queen.

There are times you might need to paint an inaccurate picture in a defender's mind.

North
♠ Q 9 7 6
♡ Q 5 4
♢ K Q J 3
♣ 8 2

West
♠ A J
♡ J 10 8
♢ 7 6 4
♣ 10 7 6 5 3

East
♠ K
♡ K 9 7 6 3 2
♢ 8 5 2
♣ J 9 4

South (You)
♠ 10 8 5 4 3 2
♡ A
♢ A 10 9
♣ A K Q

You

South	West	North	East
1 ♠	pass	3 ♠	pass
6 ♠	(all pass)		

You really must do something about your bidding. Once more you get too high and you see your opponents have two guaranteed trump tricks. West leads the ♡J. To make the hand, you need to find both the ace and king of spades as singletons — or to induce a defensive error. Can you do anything to encourage such an error?

The best chance is to cover the ♡J lead with the ♡Q, capturing East's king with your ace. Next cash the ♢A; then lead a low spade.

Thinking that the ♢A was a singleton, some Wests might rise with the ♠A to cash a heart winner before you take a pitch on dummy's diamonds. Again, the most important point is that *they won't go wrong if you don't help them a little.*

125

There is a corollary to this type of play. In 1989 I entered a tip in the annual Bols Bridge Tips competition, run by the International Bridge Press Association. The gist of my tip was this: *When they don't cover an honor, they don't have it.*

If the honor isn't covered by a defender, declarer should place the key higher honor in the other hand. But there are a few provisos:

1. The length must be in the concealed hand.

2. The declarer should not be known to have special length or strength in the suit.

3. The honor in the dummy should not be touching another honor (e.g., Q-J combination does not apply).

4. The pips in the suit should be solid enough to make it possible for you to overtake your honor without costing a trick when the suit breaks badly.

This was a typical example:

South dealer
East-West vulnerable

North
♠ K Q 3 2
♡ A 4 3
◊ J 4
♣ K J 6 5

☐

South (You)
♠ A 4
♡ 6 5 2
◊ A K 10 9 8 6
♣ 10 7

You			
South	West	North	East
1 NT*	pass	2 ♣	pass
2 ◊	pass	3 NT	(all pass)

1 NT = 12-14 points.

You decide to start with a slightly offbeat one notrump. West leads the ♡7, and you duck two rounds and win the third round in the dummy. Now you call for the ◊ J. When East plays low smoothly, it is likely he doesn't have the queen, so put up the king and cash the ace, bringing down the queen and claim 10 tricks.

Here is the layout:

North
♠ K Q 3 2
♡ A 4 3
◇ J 4
♣ K J 6 5

West
♠ 9 7 5
♡ K J 9 7
◇ Q 5
♣ A 9 4 3

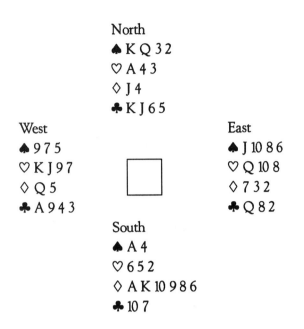

East
♠ J 10 8 6
♡ Q 10 8
◇ 7 3 2
♣ Q 8 2

South
♠ A 4
♡ 6 5 2
◇ A K 10 9 8 6
♣ 10 7

The percentage addicts would finesse the ◇J and go down.

Roll over, Houdini, the magicians are coming!

8

Swing High, Swing Low

I was introduced to golf by the Italian superstar Benito Garozzo. Immediately I became addicted. I foolishly bet him that after a year at the game I would beat him playing off a 15 handicap (he plays off 24). Me and my big mouth. In spite of the help of an attractive lady golf pro whose swing was irresistible, I lost the bet.

I find a lot of similarities in golf and bridge. In both games the right mental attitude and confidence can work to help you perform better, physically or mentally. The major difference is the attitude of players toward each other. Bridge once had the image of a refined game for gentle people — but no more. The popular conception in today's bridge world is two furious people tearing each other's hair out. Sadly, this is too often a true depiction. It's easy to forget the aim is enjoyment for everyone. Bridge partners, especially good players, are not meant to bully the weaker ones. Yet they do.

This is not so in golf, where good players often take time out to encourage, advise and sympathize with the "hackers."

Golf is a very humbling experience; it's difficult to be arrogant when you can't hit the ball. So if you have an unsympathetic bridge partner, try taking him out on the golf course. He might learn a lesson.

When I started playing and reading about bridge, I dreamed about partnering one of the great players, perhaps even one of the legendary Blue Team. It had never occurred to me that the partnership would be on the golf course. But that morning I was playing with Garozzo.

Disaster — we played badly and lost comfortably. Notwithstanding the usual civilized golf behavior, Garozzo is as famous for his competitive nature as his temper, and I spent my time avoiding his barrage of choice Neapolitan abuse as well as his hurled golf clubs. If nothing else, the outing enriched my vocabulary of Italian slang.

I was happy to get back to the hotel, to the safety of the one-armed bandits. They only wanted to rob me, not kill me. But at least I was ready to play bridge. Game time was 1 p.m. and I was well in time. The second day of the qualifying stage is different from the first in that people near the top of the field try to maintain their positions by playing down the middle and avoiding risks, while those at the back of the pack start swinging, hoping to make up lost ground.

Swinging is a term used in duplicate bridge to describe taking unusual actions. The theory is that a poorly-placed player can only make up ground by doing something different from the leaders. Swinging, more often than not, ends up unsuccessful, being by definition anti-percentage bridge. Often swinging and overbidding are closely related, and the natural tendency is to go to extremes. This is manifested by actions like doubling too much, preempting wildly, and overbidding to hopeless contracts when holding unsuitable hands. The result of such hyper-action more often than not is that the practitioner falls even further behind.

However, sensible swinging, if that isn't a paradox, can be an art, entailing subtlety and psychology rather than brute force. Here are a few suggestions that should prove useful in various forms of duplicate.

1. In team matches, the players on the leading team often anticipate that the other team will come out swinging, so they decide to keep pace by overbidding also. Fool them: Go the other way, playing conservatively, even underbidding in close situations.

2. Play different methods from your competition. For example, if the opponents use a 15-17 one-notrump opening bid, try playing 12-14, the weak notrump. Your results will automatically vary.

While doing this, try to work out what will be happening at the other tables. For example, you pick up:

♠ A 9 5 ♡ Q 8 5 4 ◇ — ♣ Q 10 9 7 6 3

Your partner opens with a weak notrump. How do you plan the auction?

If the field is playing strong notrumps, the bidding at other tables will begin with one club or one diamond. And if there is a 4-4 heart fit, it will be located immediately. But if you are looking for a swing, you would do better to give up on the heart fit. Instead, bail out into three clubs by whichever method you employ. You can be sure few pairs will have reached this contract.

3. Swing in the card-play rather than in the bidding. For example, how would you play this suit?

Dummy

♣ K 9 4 3

Declarer

♣ A J 8 5 2

The normal percentage play is to lead out the ace and king, hoping to drop the queen. But you can swing gently by taking a finesse for the queen.

Or, how about this one?

Dummy

♣ 8 5 4

Declarer

♣ A K J 7 3

In a more desperate situation, play to drop the doubleton queen offside, instead of taking the finesse like the other declarers.

4. Look for slightly unusual leads that could work out. For example, you pick up:

♠ Q 9 8 7 ♡ 6 4 3 ◇ K 5 4 ♣ 8 6 2

On lead against three notrump after an unrevealing auction of one notrump-three notrump, try the effect of leading a heart rather than the more routine spade.

5. Preemptive styles can affect results, so try to adopt a different one from your opponents.

6. Adopt swing tactics like sandbagging, which is the art of bidding slowly with big distributional hands.

Back to the game. That last point makes me wince. I was playing steadily, avoiding the flak from the more desperate competitors, when I picked up this hand:

♠ A 9 4 2   ♡ A J 8 3   ◊ 10 4   ♣ Q 6 2

At unfavorable vulnerability, the auction started:

			Zia
West	North	East	South
1 ◊	1 ♠	2 ◊	3 ◊*
4 ◊	pass	5 ◊	?

3 ◊ = a limit raise or better, in spades.

What would you do now?

Don't answer. Before you reply to any bridge question like this, always ask who your opponent is.
So who was East? OK, I'll tell you. He was Bobby Levin, a James Dean look-alike and a top-class player.
What do you do?

At the table I doubled, a bad action for many reasons, not least of all the result, which was minus 800! East had been at it and I fell right into his trap. He redoubled and then made the contract (800 under the new scoring that has been in effect since 1987, awarding a 100-point bonus for making a redoubled contract).
This was the full deal:

West dealer
North-South vulnerable

North
♠ K J 10 6 5
♡ 7 6 2
◊ 8
♣ K J 5 4

West
♠ Q 8 7 3
♡ K Q 5
◊ A K 7 6 2
♣ 8

East (Levin)
♠ —
♡ 10 9 4
◊ Q J 9 5 3
♣ A 10 9 7 3

South (Zia)
♠ A 9 4 2
♡ A J 8 3
◊ 10 4
♣ Q 6 2

		Levin	Zia
West	North	East	South
1 ◊	1 ♠	2 ◊	3 ◊
4 ◊	pass	5 ◊	double
pass	pass	redouble	(all pass)

I should never have doubled, but give full credit to Levin
for his simple two-diamond raise. This is a good example of
a way in which a player can generate a swing.

Here's a more difficult one.

To set the scene, you're in one of the early rounds of the
Vanderbilt (one of the major North American national team
championships). Your opposition is top class, and with 16
boards to go, you are trailing by an even 40 imps. The good
news is that you have started a rally and feel that with one

134

more good result, you might just be out of trouble. The bad news is there are only two boards to go — you're running out of time. However, you suddenly pick up a hand containing a void. A void is always a green light, a chance to get moving.

♠ 10 9 3 2 ♡ 8 2 ◇ — ♣ K Q J 10 9 7 6

You are East at favorable vulnerability. The auction starts like this:

South	West	North	East
1 NT*	pass	2 ◇	?

1 NT = 15-17 points
2 ◇ = transfer to hearts

What do you bid?

Most bridge players have a habit of bidding first and thinking later. Your reaction might be to bid anything from three clubs to six clubs. Think ahead — that's what will happen in the other room. Remember, you need a swing. If you jump in clubs, your left-hand opponent will pass, right-hand opponent will bid his hearts and you will end up on lead against some number of hearts.

But you don't want to be on lead. You want your partner to be on lead so you can ruff a diamond. You must allow your left-hand opponent to bid hearts first. The correct bid is pass. Let your left-hand opponent bid hearts. Let your right-hand opponent bid his game or slam. Then double for a diamond lead and win the match. Congratulations — you are a swinger.

* * * * * * * * *

For the rest of the Individual session, things went well, and when play finished I was confident that I had qualified.

This was not in itself such a big deal, but accidents do happen, and a surprising number of top players did fail to make the cut. In fact, when the results were posted I had moved up to a comfortable fifth.

The first step was over. Tomorrow the final would begin, but for now we could relax. The leaders were mostly familiar names, with the majority, perhaps 80 percent of the 40 qualifiers, being men. To be fair, however, only a small percentage of the original entrants were women. The few women represented were the best and would hold their own. But why did so few women enter the event?

This is a delicate question. If you asked the best players to make a list of the top 100 players in the world today, not one of them would include the name of a woman — sad but true. However, the old-timers would have had the late U.S. champion Helen Sobel high on their list.

This fact would be agreed to by all the men and even most of the women: Today, bridge at the top is all men. Why? There are two main theories. The first, held mainly by women but also by some men, is that women have traditionally not had the same opportunities as men. They have not had the time to devote to the game, but also they are conditioned by society to believe that they cannot compete successfully with men. They aren't given the chance to play enough at the top levels. They are not included in the men's teams, and by playing in women's events, as opposeed to open tournaments, they aren't given the chance to improve and fulfill their maximum potential. The proponents of this view believe that, given the same opportunities, women could compete to an equally high standard.

The opposing view is that women are made differently from men, their physiological compositions being less suited for whatever it takes to be a top bridge player. Proponents of the second view do not feel that these differences make women less competent than men in other fields, only in specific areas which draw on particular skills, chess and poker being further examples.*

I have to agree with the second group. My women friends tell me I am chauvinistic. They are probably right, but I don't think I am being so here. I do genuinely feel that women can perform most intellectual activities as well or even better than men. I believe, for instance, that women's inherent qualities as leaders are undoubtedly at least equal to men. But men and women are different, and the world is not always a logical place when it comes to the sexes.

Perhaps a friend of mine, the reputed psychologist from the University of Pennsylvania, Marty Seligman, has the real answer. He maintains that one of the ingredients that goes into making a top player is the male hormone, testosterone. It is found more in men than in women. This might explain the dilemma.

I haven't got the courage to discuss this subject any further — it's far too explosive. But I feel that if argument number one were correct, there would be at least a few isolated instances of a woman being up there with the men.

Be that as it may, it seems that this question will be answered in the near future, because American women bridge players, most unhappy with the status quo, have rebelled.

Jill Blanchard, a top woman player, took the American Contract Bridge League (ACBL) to court to force them to stop holding segregated men's and women's events, and to open up men's events to anyone regardless of sex.

Jill first decided that she wanted to play in open events after the following incident. She was playing with her mother, Gail Greenberg, who is many times a world champion in women's events. They had bid well to a contract of seven clubs. The contract had gone down because of a bad

---

* Note all my intellectual examples are games rather than professions.

break in a side suit, and Gail told Jill, "Don't you know you don't bid grand slams in women's events, even if it's the best contract. You get a good enough score just bidding six."

Gail was right; they scored terribly because no one else had bid to the good grand slam. And if they had bid six, they would have scored over average.

The whole affair infuriated Jill, who thought it was ridiculous that to do well in women's bridge the recommended action was to play "badly." She won the court case, and now in North America there are no tournaments restricted to men. In 1990, by beating the top males, Jill won the right to take part in the playoffs to select the 1991 American Bermuda Bowl world championship team. Her squad contained three men and three women, the first time more than one woman had been on a trials team. They didn't win, but they did a lot to boost women's morale.

9

Table Presents and Table Presence

Atlantic City, Tuesday Evening

A group of us had dinner at the hotel. Tim hadn't qualified for the final, but the Weasel, still complaining, was comfortably in. Tim wasn't worried, however, because he had an alternative attraction. He told us over dinner of a backgammon game he had planned for the evening — one of the common perks of tournaments — and of the interesting situation he had fixed up.

He would play 10 matches of one game each with his opponent. The stake would vary, and the interesting part was that neither of them would know what it was until the game was over. One of them would place a dollar bill under the board before each game. After the game, they would remove the bill; the stake would be the last four figures on the note. Thus the stake was a minimum of nothing (usually, however, at least $1,000) and a maximum of $9,999! No wonder he wasn't too concerned at being out of the final. His opponent was Louie, a successful sports better and bookmaker from

New York. Louie was also a fine backgammon player and was accustomed to big action. The game figured to be good watching, but Louie likes privacy when he plays. We would have to hear later about the results.

Table Presence

Everyone remembers how he learned to play bridge. Part of that learning process is playing with better players, and I, too, followed this route — paying for the privilege on occasion. As I progressed, moving up in stakes periodically, perhaps the most important lesson of all was not to be involved in the emotion of winning and losing, recognizing that both were inevitable and that they interfered with judgment. This was a difficulty, but after a while I became almost immune to the results. It is vital to be detached when gambling.

There were other lessons. The top players had individual traits from which I could learn. They also had common traits, which every bridge player should master. To become a complete bridge player, you need a mixture of qualities — some worked for, some acquired, and others innate.

Card sense is the most obvious talent of the gifted player. This is an innate ability, but if you aren't born with a body full of card sense, you can still "learn" about cards. The players with card sense enjoy a familiarity and ease with the cards. Often they "know" how the cards lie. All the great players have it.

Another quality that is partly innate and partly acquired is *table presence.*

Have you ever known that an opponent was going to make a particular bid even before he made it? Have you ever felt sure that someone, either your partner or an opponent, was about to play a specific card, and he did? Have you ever sensed that a key suit was going to break badly, and you were right? Or, have you ever wanted to double the opponents for no good reason, decided against it, and cursed later when they went several down?

It's possible that at each of these times you were using psychic gifts, which allow you to look into the future. But it is very unlikely. There may be a place for magic, but it isn't at the bridge table. It is much more likely that, without knowing it, you were using table presence.

For years table presence has been part of the private domain of the expert. It is a mysterious, charismatic quality that allows demigods at the bridge table to dazzle and delight. One moment they locate a missing queen or jack, the next they make an inspired bid in an apparently hopeless situation. And when a mere mortal asked for the explanation of the bid or play, the answer is always the same: table presence.

Yet nobody has ever explained table presence. What exactly is it? Where do you find it? How do you keep it? Is it catching?

Relax, I am about to tell you. Table presence is simply a term used to describe the way a player knows or feels what's happening around the table. One inch under the atmosphere around every table, there's an invisible screen on which a movie is continually being played. Modest people don't know it's there, but the successful player is one who can see it, hear it and feel it.

You are in a grand slam, the moment of truth arrives and you have to guess this combination in order to catch the queen:

Dummy
♠ A 10 4

☐

You
♠ K J 7

Can you recall the tenseness and anticipation around the table? Reading that atmosphere correctly is one of the most valuable talents in bridge. But it isn't easy to come by. There are few who can really read the table. One of these was P. Hal Sims. He was an American player who boasted that he had never misguessed a two-way finesse for a queen. He would always "smell" it out, and was prepared to put money where his mouth was. To test him, a friend once fixed a hand, putting Sims into a grand slam in which he had to guess a two-way finesse in spades.

After thinking for some time, Sims leapt out of his chair, shouting, "This is impossible. You've both got the queen!" And he was right!

Acquiring table presence isn't as difficult as it seems. Suppose declarer opens with a strong notrump and his partner raises to three notrump. You make a lead and dummy comes down with a 13-count.

At this point, on most occasions, a defender can relax because the contract is probably going to be easy. But if you see the declarer, who has a minimum of 28 points between the two hands, taking a long time to play, *wake up*. He's obviously got a problem. It's no time to relax. That's table presence.

You open one notrump and partner gives you three notrump. Your left-hand opponent takes a long time to lead. That's already interesting. He's unlikely to have a five-card suit, unless he has a very weak hand with no entry and is trying to find his partner's long suit. Play the hand accordingly. That's table presence.

When an opponent hesitates, you should try to work out why he is pausing (though remember always that you do this at your own risk). However, it is totally impermissible to purposely try to mislead an opponent by hesitating, or to take advantage of information gleaned from your own partner's pause.

A slow raise of an invitation usually means a minimum, a quick raise a maximum. We've all heard happy and sad bids. Often you can tell what your opponent holds. If you haven't been doing it, start registering such information and using it. This is another example of table presence. Feeling the mood of your opponent and trying to understand what he's thinking and why, are winning tactics. It can look magical at times, too.

Once I was playing against a top expert in an international event. He thought for several seconds longer than usual before opening one notrump. I scribbled on a piece of paper: "Your distribution is 2-4-5-2,"* which it was.

I hadn't peeked at his hand, and I'll admit I was a bit lucky. Here's how my thoughts went: He's opened one notrump, but there's something unusual about his hand. Most players are strict about their point-count requirements; the likelihood is that he is off-shape. Opening one notrump with a six-card minor is common practice, so if that had been his problem, he would have solved it quicker. He is probably some 5-4-2-2, and was debating whether to reverse or to open one notrump. With a five-card major, surely he would open in that suit. So his long suit must be minor.

My hand was:

---

* Two spades, four hearts, five diamonds and two clubs.

♠ A J 6 5   ♡ 10 7   ◇ 9 4   ♣ A Q 6 5 2

It was likely he had length in my short suits (i.e., four hearts and five diamonds).

As you can see, the reasoning wasn't complicated, it was an example of table presence. Of course, showing off verbally to an expert isn't recommended practice — he might use *his* table presence to figure out how you knew his shape, and work out *your* black-suit length.

Were you ever clutching ♠Q-x-x and the opponents bid all the way to seven spades? Can you recall trying to look bored when your partner started to ask questions about the bidding? No doubt you felt terrible, sure that the questions would alert the declarer, who would pick up your queen. No one would ask a lot of questions when looking at the queen of trumps with the opponents in seven.

Well, remember that the next time *you* are the declarer. That's *table presence*.

Every rule has an exception, and I'm still trying to forget this one from a friendly game. I was declarer in seven clubs with this trump suit:

Dummy

♣ A 4 3

Declarer (Zia)

♣ K J 9 5 2

Not the best grand. The dummy had been tabled and I was about to cash the ace and follow with the finesse of the jack, when my right-hand opponent started asking a string of questions about the bidding. I was sure he couldn't have the

♣Q. I won the first trick in hand and led the ♣J. Wrong! He won with the queen, from ♣Q-x-x. He was just a beginner and genuinely curious about the auction. He hadn't reached the stage where he would become too nervous to ask.

He Who Hesitates is Last

It's hard to list the rules regarding this subject. Every situation is different. The one crucial point is: Honest people always hesitate for a reason and your job is to work out why. Try this. After a heavy day at the office, you pick up a fair hand:

♠ 8 4   ♡ K 6 5   ◊ A 8 3   ♣ A Q J 9 2

There are two passes to you and, though you have only 14 points, you opt to open a 15-17-point one notrump because you like the look of your ♣9. Your left-hand opponent, a sweet LOL (Little Old Lady) who always has her bid, overcalls two spades.

Partner bids three spades, which is Stayman in this sequence. You don't have a spade stopper or four hearts, so you continue with a natural four clubs.

After a pass by the LOL, your partner says, "Points, shmoints," and leaps to six clubs!

In spite of your minimum your hand is beginning to look quite good. LOL passes after a slight pause, and then leads the ♠K.

This is what you can see:

North dealer
All vulnerable

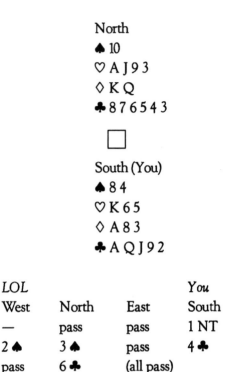

North
♠ 10
♡ A J 9 3
◊ K Q
♣ 8 7 6 5 4 3

South (You)
♠ 8 4
♡ K 6 5
◊ A 8 3
♣ A Q J 9 2

LOL			You
West	North	East	South
—	pass	pass	1 NT
2 ♠	3 ♠	pass	4 ♣
pass	6 ♣	(all pass)	

You've both overbid a little but the dummy is about par, the ◊ Q being the only wasted card. You lost a spade trick, which makes the trump play crucial. You also have a heart problem.

At trick two West switches to a diamond. You win in the dummy and lead a trump, East contributing the 10. It's time to guess trumps. Do you finesse or play for the drop?

In the absence of outside information, playing for the drop and finessing are close. The actual percentages are 52 percent for playing the ace and 50 percent for finessing.

What clues do we have?

146

Let's start with the spade position. West seems to have six or seven to the ace-king-queen, because if East had three or four spades to the queen, he probably would have doubled the three-spade cuebid to show support. That's not much help.

There is not much we can deduce about the rest of the distribution, except perhaps to focus on West's slight pause at the end of the auction. Problems are often best tackled by putting yourself in the place of the other person.

Suppose as West you had something like this:

♠ A K Q x x x ♡ x x x ◇ x x x ♣ K

What would you do over six clubs? That's easy — you'd pass, quickly (perhaps pulling your cards closer to your chest). Yes, West would have no problem if she held the ♣K. She must have been considering a sacrifice of six spades. That surely means she's void in clubs.

Happy that you were awake enough to pick up the pause, you finesse the ♣Q. As expected, West shows out. Justice is served when the heart finesse is on as well, allowing you to pick up the slam bonus.

These were the East-West cards:

West	East
♠ A K Q 7 6 5 3	♠ J 9 2
♡ Q 8 2	♡ 10 7 4
◇ J 7 2	◇ 10 9 6 5 4
♣ —	♣ K 10

Swedish Delight

Now that you've got the hang of table presence, join me in Stockholm at the 1983 World Championships. As usual you're on center stage. Sitting South, you pick up a beauty:

147

♠ A K 2 ♡ A K Q 10 8 ◊ — ♣ A Q 9 7 4

The bidding proceeds:

You			
South	West	North	East
2♣*	pass	2◊*	double*
2♡	pass	3◊	pass
4♣	double	5♣	pass
5♠	pass	6♡	(all pass)

2♣ = strong, artificial and forcing

2◊ = negative

East's double = diamonds

After a confusing auction, during which West has asked innumerable questions, he leads the ◊8, which is covered by the jack and king. This is what you can see:

North
♠ J 10 4 3
♡ J 3 2
◊ Q J 7 5 4 2
♣ —

☐

South
♠ A K 2
♡ A K Q 10 8
◊ —
♣ A Q 9 7 4

That is a disappointing dummy, but for now your problem is to make six hearts, not to comment on partner's overbidding. What is your plan?

It's a complicated hand, and you probably need the hearts to be 3-2. The normal line must be to cash the ♣A, and play to ruff three clubs in dummy. If the ♣K comes down in three rounds or the clubs are 4-4, you are home; otherwise you can try the spade finesse.

However, West's double of four clubs and his questions have changed the situation. Remember table presence! Here, when East shows up with the ◊A-K, it becomes likely that West has both missing black honors: the ♣K and ♠Q.

Proceeding on this assumption, you ruff the diamond lead, ruff a club (without cashing the ace), play a spade to the ace, and ruff a second club. A spade to the king is followed by a third club ruff. You trump a diamond in hand, arriving at this position:

North
♠ J 10
♡ —
◊ Q 7 5 4
♣ —

South (you)
♠ 2
♡ A K Q
◊ —
♣ A Q

It's time to draw trumps, and West follows to three rounds. Now you exit with your last spade, endplaying West to lead into your ♣A-Q.

Nicely done! This was the hand:

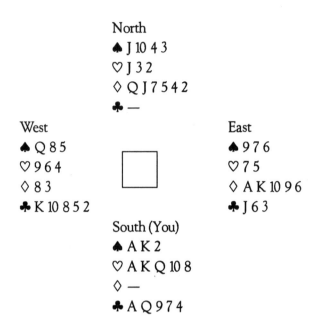

North
♠ J 10 4 3
♡ J 3 2
◇ Q J 7 5 4 2
♣ —

West
♠ Q 8 5
♡ 9 6 4
◇ 8 3
♣ K 10 8 5 2

East
♠ 9 7 6
♡ 7 5
◇ A K 10 9 6
♣ J 6 3

South (You)
♠ A K 2
♡ A K Q 10 8
◇ —
♣ A Q 9 7 4

Playing West for the ♠Q, you would succeed even if West started with four spades and only two hearts. He would have been forced to discard a low spade on the third round of hearts.

Another aspect of table presence is anticipating the likely result of the contract. When defending, if you think the contract will make, look for a chance to deflect declarer from the winning line.

You're involved in a tough 64-board match. You've pulled ahead of your opponents. You hold:

♠ A 8 7 6 4 3 ♡ A K ◇ A K Q 5 ♣ A

This strong hand, with its long weak suit, is hard enough to bid given a free run, but here West opens with a bid of three clubs. You do what you can, leading to this auction:

	West	North	East	*You*
				South
	3 ♣	pass	pass	4 ♣*
	pass	4 ♡	pass	5 ♠
	pass	6 ♠	(all pass)	

4 ♣ = a very powerful hand.

West leads the ♣K, and the dummy comes down to the amusement of the kibitzers:

Dummy
♠ Q 10 9
♡ 6 5 4 2
◊ 6 3 2
♣ 8 6 5

☐

Declarer (You)
♠ A 8 7 6 4 3
♡ A K
◊ A K Q 5
♣ A

The kibitzers are wrong. Your five spades begged partner to raise with any help. He judged well to bid the slam, but you need something favorable to happen in spades. You win the first trick with the ♣A and cash the ♠A (it goes: jack, 9, 5). That's revealing — West seems to have started with a singleton spade. You can now test the diamonds, ruffing the fourth round if they don't break. (If East ruffs the third round, you never had a chance.) To your surprise, West ruffs the queen of diamonds with the ♠2.
This was the hand:

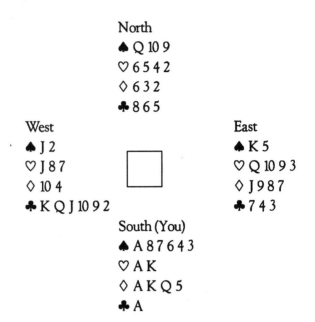

North
♠ Q 10 9
♡ 6 5 4 2
◇ 6 3 2
♣ 8 6 5

West
♠ J 2
♡ J 8 7
◇ 10 4
♣ K Q J 10 9 2

East
♠ K 5
♡ Q 10 9 3
◇ J 9 8 7
♣ 7 4 3

South (You)
♠ A 8 7 6 4 3
♡ A K
◇ A K Q 5
♣ A

West made a fine play when he threw the ♠J. Left to your own devices, you would have played the ace and another spade, making when the trumps broke 2-2. The falsecard was simple yet effective. Most people don't realize that it's often right to drop a high card a round early. For example, assume that declarer is in a spade contract, and this is the trump layout:

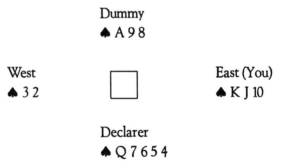

Dummy
♠ A 9 8

West
♠ 3 2

East (You)
♠ K J 10

Declarer
♠ Q 7 6 5 4

You are entitled to one trick only. If you throw the ♠K under the ace, you'll still get one trick, but South, thinking that the suit is breaking 4-1, may abandon trumps and lose another trick later. Similarly:

Dummy

♠ Q 10 7 4 2

West (You)   East

♠ K 3   ♠ J 9 6

Declarer

♠ A 8 5

Again, your side is due to get only one spade trick, but if you jettison the king under the ace, declarer might stop playing the suit.

* * * * * * * * *

Back in the hotel casino, Sarah Jane seemed to be off duty. Her replacement was an unfriendly man, who for some reason annoyed me by the way he pulled the cards out of the shoe. In addition, he belonged to that sadistic clan of croupiers who seem to take great pleasure in winning from the players. He was so unsympathetic that I didn't stay long.

The casino was less lively than the previous day, and I noticed that Omar Sharif was nowhere to be seen. The official word was that he wasn't feeling well, but the inside gossip was that he was unhappy with the casino and was staying away from the tables.

On the way back to my room, I passed the results board, where a few die-hards were still checking their scores. Errors can occur. In the semifinal of the 1990 World Championship in Geneva, the Canadians lost their match to the German team because of a recording error. The German team went on to win the Championship.

I tried to think about the next day's play, but I found that the adrenalin hadn't started to flow. I still wasn't into the excitement — there would be time enough tomorrow.

153

10

Tall Oaks from Little Acorns Grow

Rye Town, New York, October 1981

We had really made it; the Pakistan team had qualified to play in the Bermuda Bowl in Rye, some 20 miles north of Manhattan. We were on a high. The good news was that we were about to participate in our first world championship. The players were excited, and even a few members of the public had started taking an interest in our existence — a good sign. On the down-side was the fact that our presence added a new dimension to the meaning of the word "underdog." More than a few whispers were heard to the effect that we were bringing down the standard of the event and even that we shouldn't be there. Too bad. It was true that we didn't expect to do well, but the experience had to be good for us, and we hoped that our taking part would promote the game in Pakistan. If nothing else, we could show that we knew a thing or two about sportsmanship.

Everybody was tipping the strong American squad as favorites. They were all new names to us, but that wasn't surprising. Most of the people whose names we would recognize, Culbertson, Goren, and so on, vanished years ago. This time the team included the latest American killing machine: Jeff Meckstroth and Eric Rodwell, two young players reputed to possess an affinity for mercilessly destroying the opponents.

Apart from America, Poland and Great Britain were likely to pose the biggest threat — the British team included some of my rubber bridge friends from the old days in London: Rose, Sheehan and Collings, now enemies at the table. At least I would know their styles of play when we met them, whatever that would be worth. The rest of the field seemed impressive too, with strong teams from South America and the Far East. No one seemed able to even get our names right, mixing our first and family names almost at random!

The pundits said we had no hope. The journalists said we had no hope. Even the players agreed we had no hope — that is, except for "Chance."

There's an optimist in every group, on every team. Chance was ours. Long ago we called him Chance (his real name is Nisar) because of his adventurous bidding style and his never-say-die attitude — no team was too tough for him. The very thought of losing was preposterous.

"Just let me sit at the table against them," he would assert when the Americans were mentioned. "I'll deal with them." Then as proof of his prowess, he would quote some hand from the past where he pulled off a devilish coup. "See," he added confidently, "I'll make *Keema* (mincemeat) of them."

I must admit that I liked his attitude, even though his dreams seemed more fantasy than reality. I could even agree that our players might be able to hold their own in card-play, but I knew in my heart that it wouldn't be enough.

Bridge had changed in the last decade, especially at the top. Unlike the early days, high-level games had become much more of a bidding competition. Highly sophisticated methods had taken over from judgment and card skills. Here we were pitifully outgunned. We were all using old-fashioned Acol, by comparison a simple but antiquated system. Acol is fine for a friendly game at home, but compared to the science of our opponents, it was a bit like fighting nuclear weapons with a bow and arrow. In addition, some of the other players, the Americans, for instance, were full-time professionals who played regularly against top-class opposition. We were casual amateurs — a big difference. Our team played irregularly at best.

Where others were preparing vigorously for the competition, combining physical training with twentieth-century technology, even working with computer printouts of their own and opponents' methods, our group was predictably much more casual. Our biggest challenge seemed to be in making the decision of whether to spend more time buying items like jeans, artificial flowers and other presents on our long shopping lists, or chatting up the women's teams. Objectively, I felt that to do well we would need to have a prolonged spell in *Heat #1*.

Do you, as a bridge player, find that on some days you play terribly and on others really well? Have you wondered why? American theorist, Roger Stern, may have the answer. Stern maintains that it is impossible for anyone to play consistently well. We are all bound to play at different levels. There are three main categories, or *heats* as he calls them.

Heat #1

This is the magic heat. You play above yourself. You are no longer a bridge player, you're an artist, a poet. The cards respond to your touch, they fly, they sing, they come alive for you. In addition, everything, luck included, is going for you. You're invulnerable — you can't make a mistake.

Heat #2

This is your normal level or standard. You play as you would expect to: middle of the road.

Heat #3

You wish you'd stayed in bed. You play terribly and out of luck. Every finesse is wrong, every suit breaks badly. The opponents play like champions and you lose, with a capital L.

Stern asserts that if a player can be objective about his heat, he can drastically improve his results. Here's how: Each time you play, as soon as possible, carefully determine which heat you are in. Now adjust your game accordingly.

In Heat #1: Get involved, take control, make daring decisions, be strong — remember, you own the table.

In Heat #2: Plod along, do your normal thing.

In Heat #3: Beware, take a back seat. Play passively, play with caution. Whenever possible, let your partner make the key decision and stay out of the way. Just try to stay alive.

In real life, what normally happens is that when in Heat #3, players invariably try to make up for their bad results. Don't do it — things only get worse. It's almost impossible to think clearly when things are going badly. The trick is to learn not to fight this heat, but to live with it.

Stern's theory is one of the most valuable pieces of bridge advice ever given to me. I insist that all my partners and teammates follow it. I would strongly advise bridge players at all levels to use it and watch their results start improving.

Meanwhile back at the tournament my American friend Matt Granovetter agreed to act as coach. Our captain thought that this would make all the difference. Certainly it would be a psychological boost, but I wondered if *anything* really would help. The format was a double round-robin with the four teams leading after seven days playing off in the semifinals and final. Our group consisted of six players, two officials and just one supporter.

The supporter, Beroze, was unique. Lady bridge supporters are not common in our part of the world, but she's a real enthusiast, and so faithful that she had traveled all the way from Pakistan just to root for us. She never missed a match, but if it wasn't to be a wasted journey, she needed to have brought along a miracle or two.

When the tournament started, for a moment we thought she had come suitably armed, because, surprisingly, in the first match we narrowly beat the Americans.

However, we didn't have time to let this victory go to our heads. With a sickening monotony, we lost the next six matches. Disappointed, but not too surprised, at the end of the first round-robin, we found ourselves near the bottom of the pack. At the top, the bookies were losing money because Britain and America were leading.

For us, the dreaded Heat #3 seemed to be spreading its poison. Faced with a choice, we invariably did the wrong thing. Here is an example from our seventh-round match against Argentina. At unfavorable vulnerability, I picked up:

♠ Q ♡ A 10 7 6 ♢ K 4 2 ♣ K Q 9 7 6

The auction was difficult:

	Masood		*Zia*
West	North	East	South
—	—	pass	1 ♣
1 ♠	3 ◊	4 ♠	4 NT*
pass	5 ♣*	pass	5 ♡*
pass	5 NT*	pass	7 ◊! *
double*	7 NT*	(all pass)	

4 NT = Blackwood

5 ♣ = zero or three aces

5 ♡ = asking for extras, according to our system

5 NT = undiscussed; just keep the ball rolling

7 ◊ = hoping for the queen of diamonds and enough
bits and pieces

double = Lightner — he wants a club lead

7 NT = knowing that seven diamonds will go down
at trick one

West led the ♡K, and this was what I could see:

♠ A
♡ 3
◊ A J 9 8 5
♣ A J 10 8 4 2

☐

♠ Q
♡ A 10 7 6
◊ K 4 2
♣ K Q 9 7 6

The key to making the contract was the diamond suit.
After winning with the ♡A, I took three rounds of clubs, then
cashed the ◊K (3, 5, 10). I played a diamond, West contributing the 6. What would you do?

At the time, I couldn't see any reason not to make the percentage play, so I finessed dummy's jack. The roof fell in, because this was the entire deal:

North (Masood)
♠ A
♡ 3
◇ A J 9 8 5
♣ A J 10 8 4 2

West
♠ K 10 8 4 2
♡ K Q 8 5 4
◇ 7 6 3
♣ —

East
♠ J 9 7 6 5 3
♡ J 9 2
◇ Q 10
♣ 5 3

South (Zia)
♠ Q
♡ A 10 7 6
◇ K 4 2
♣ K Q 9 7 6

On reflection, I think I made a bad play. West doubled seven diamonds. Yes, he had a club void, but he also knew we might run to seven notrump. He certainly would have doubled with ◇7-6-3, but looking at ◇Q-6-3 or ◇Q-7-6-3 he might well have passed over seven diamonds, taking his chance on either getting a club lead anyway or just scoring his ◇Q. Was this a variation of restricted choice? Or the kind of hand you need to be in Heat #1 to make?

In the other room, Munir lost 500 points in six spades doubled. We dropped 14 imps on the board, instead of gaining 17 had I made the grand. Only 31 imps swinging on a guess.

Our camp was full of long faces. Even Chance was beginning to sound despondent.

Tall Oaks . . .

Help came from the least expected quarter. SAPP (an acronym for Stone-Age Acol with Paki Preempts) was a bidding system, or so they say. It was the secret weapon and brainchild of Munir, one of our team members. Munir is a Rhodes scholar, and SAPP was a complicated concoction of his brilliant, if twisted (trust me), mind.

It works more or less like any other system. Bids at the one-level were old-fashioned Acol, but at the two-level SAPP took its followers into a weird and wonderful world where all bids had multiple meanings. Bids from two clubs to four hearts were all multi-purpose. For instance, an opening bid of three clubs showed either:

- a diamond preempt (with a bad suit); or
- a heart preempt (with two of the top three honors); or
- a strong 6-4 or 7-4 in spades and hearts; or
- a solid seven-card minor with a king outside; or
- a four-heart or four-spade opener with two first-round controls, one of which may be a void.

I told you his mind was twisted — now maybe you'll believe me.

The original purpose of this system was twofold. First, to drive terror and confusion into the adversaries; and second, by playing a method that catered for the "one-in-a-million" hand, at least we'd gain when — or should I say "if" — it came up.

The results so far had been less than spectacular. The good news was that it had succeeded in creating fear and confusion. The bad news was that it filled not his opponents' mind with fear and confusion, but his partner's mind! Fazli, Munir's partner, had aged 20 years trying to remember the meanings of all the bids. None of the one-in-a-million hands had come up, so the system hadn't been tried out. Oh, we of little faith!

Along came this hand:

West	East
♠ A K J 8 7 5 4 3	♠ 9 2
♡ 7 6 3	♡ K Q 5
◊ —	◊ 8 7 4 3
♣ K 5	♣ A Q 10 7

Munir	Fazli
3 ♣*	3 ♡*
4 ♠*	5 ♣*
5 ◊*	6 ♠*
pass	

3 ♣ = the fifth hand-type, as described on page 161

3 ♡ = Knowing partner will convert, East was prepared
to play in four diamonds opposite a diamond preempt.

4 ♠ = extra length, a maximum and slammish hand

5 ♣ = cuebid

5 ◊ = cuebid

6 ♠ = Bingo!

Naturally every other human being opened four spades
and played there. We picked up a slam swing and won the
match. There were two consequences. The first was that
Munir was thrilled. For the next few days, he could be found
regularly expounding his bidding theories to anybody who
would listen — usually the waitresses in the coffee shop
(although there were rumors that he had ulterior motives).

The second consequence was that, as if by magic, the
floodgates opened. Suddenly we were on a roll and the whole
team stepped into Heat #1. When an aggressive player gets
going, he really goes. Take Chance. At the table, he invented
a sequence that even I'd never heard of before — or since.
Sitting South, he picked up this hand:

♠ 8 3 ♡ A Q 9 ◇ J 10 7 6 4 ♣ A 9 2

			Chance
West	North	East	South
—	—	pass	pass
1 ♠	pass	pass	double*
pass	1 NT	pass	2 NT*
pass	3 NT*	(all pass)	

double = normal protecting double
2 NT = The impossible bid: raise à la Chance
3 NT = Nishat, Chance's partner, is used to such
sequences.

Madness, genius, inspiration — I don't know. I do know
that three notrump made. Heat #1 can be infectious! But first:
confession time. People think that experts always plan every
move or play they make well in advance. They certainly try
to, and thinking ahead is fundamental, but the truth is that
many times a good declarer or defender just falls into the
right line — a mixture of luck and technique. In Heat #1 this
happens more often than normally.

OK, lecture over, try this:

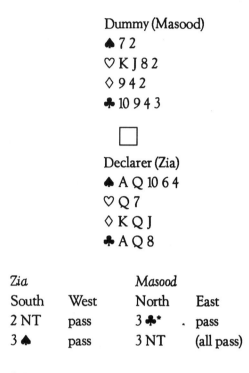

Dummy (Masood)
♠ 7 2
♡ K J 8 2
◇ 9 4 2
♣ 10 9 4 3

Declarer (Zia)
♠ A Q 10 6 4
♡ Q 7
◇ K Q J
♣ A Q 8

Zia		Masood	
South	West	North	East
2 NT	pass	3 ♣*	. pass
3 ♠	pass	3 NT	(all pass)

3 ♣ = Stayman

The match was against the Poles, and the guy on my left (West), a fine player with an unpronounceable name, led the ♡10, showing something or other. I didn't ask; I was too busy trying to form a plan. Anyway, how would you proceed?

Looking at the dummy, my thoughts went something like this: "Not a great contract — the bidding is normal, but the hands fit badly. Where do I start? I'd like to play spades and clubs at the same time, and both from the dummy, but I am in danger of never getting there.

"It seems likely that West doesn't have a long suit or he wouldn't have led a heart. He knew from the bidding that dummy has four of them. Probably he has honors in the other suits, or he might have been more aggressive.

"This hand is taking too long. Sooner or later I'll have to

do something with the spades, so I'd better start there. No particular play looks appealing, but if West has the ♠K, leading the queen out of my hand won't cost."

I played low from the dummy at trick one, as did East, and won in hand with the ♡Q. I then led the ♠Q, which West won with the king. At least I hadn't wasted my time trying to get into the dummy to take a finesse that was going to lose.

West switched to a diamond; East won the ace and returned a second diamond. Next I played a heart to the jack, West following with the *nine*. East won with the ♡A and led a third diamond. From the spots, it looked like he had the 13th diamond. With three tricks each, this was the position:

Dummy
♠ 7
♡ K 8
♢ —
♣ 10 9 4 3

□

Declarer
♠ A 10 6 4
♡ —
♢ —
♣ A Q 8

Now what?

Once more, I paused to consider: "West seems to have started with two hearts, three diamonds and a lot of black cards. With five clubs he would have led one, so he's probably 4-4 or 5-3 in spades and clubs. In either case, playing spades is hopeless. That leaves clubs. If East has the ♣K, I've no chance, because he'll cash his diamond. So I'll play West for it.

"I still can't see how I'm going to make this hand, but at least I can maintain symmetry by playing another black queen out of my hand."

I didn't know it then, but this was the actual position around the table:

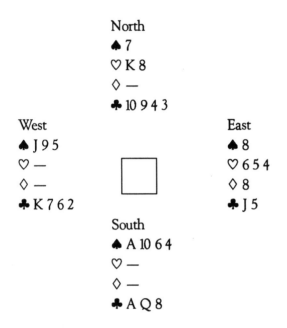

North
♠ 7
♡ K 8
♢ —
♣ 10 9 4 3

West
♠ J 9 5
♡ —
♢ —
♣ K 7 6 2

East
♠ 8
♡ 6 5 4
♢ 8
♣ J 5

South
♠ A 10 6 4
♡ —
♢ —
♣ A Q 8

I led the ♣Q from my hand. To defeat the contract, West had to duck his king, but West made a mistake by winning the trick. Remember, we were in Heat #1, where *opponents* make the mistakes; and East had already erred by failing to hold up his ♢A for two rounds. West played back a club.

It looked as though I had to play low from dummy and hope for a doubleton ♣J to win nine tricks. But that wasn't true. There was a much sexier line. I put up the ♣10, winning East's jack with the ace. I played a club to dummy's 9, and cashed my two heart winners, squeezing West in spades and clubs. He had to bare his ♠J, so at the twelfth trick I led a spade to my ace, dropping his jack!

It looked good and felt great! This was the full hand:

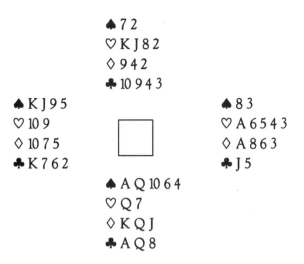

```
                    ♠ 7 2
                    ♡ K J 8 2
                    ◊ 9 4 2
                    ♣ 10 9 4 3
    ♠ K J 9 5                      ♠ 8 3
    ♡ 10 9                         ♡ A 6 5 4 3
    ◊ 10 7 5                       ◊ A 8 6 3
    ♣ K 7 6 2                      ♣ J 5
                    ♠ A Q 10 6 4
                    ♡ Q 7
                    ◊ K Q J
                    ♣ A Q 8
```

Boom! We won the next three matches and started gathering in the points, clawing our way up the pack.

We started getting excited. Some of the spectators started asking, "Who are these guys?" We became encouraged enough to start calculating the number of points needed to get to the semifinals. We actually started listening to our coach.

We even talked about having early nights (just talk, that idea was soon rejected). Actually, early nights in themselves aren't always enough. Anybody who has played a lot of bridge can tell you that regardless of how exhausted you are, it isn't easy to sleep after a tough game. More likely as you lie in bed, the ghosts of recently played hands come out to haunt you, whirling around inside your consciousness.

First come the most painful deals: the misses — misbids, misplays, missed inferences and mistakes. You curse yourself for your stupidities. If you manage to push these thoughts away, you can turn your mind to the good moments.

There isn't a player in existence who doesn't sooner or later recall his triumphs. Who can resist the indulgence of lingering on a beautiful moment? I know I can't. To tell you the truth, I love these hands and looked forward to the nocturnal pleasure of savoring the remembrance of a good play or bid. But it's hard to play well when you are tired, so sometimes when you're really exhausted, the only way to get a good night's sleep is to take a sleeping pill.

Yet even that isn't always enough. I remember one evening near the end of the second round-robin. We had two or three matches to play and, needing a good rest, I had gone to bed early. About two in the morning I was awakened by an insistent knocking on the door. When I realized it wouldn't go away, I opened the door to find a smiling if tipsy blonde with two glasses of brandy clutched precariously in her hands. I recognized her from one of the cocktail parties earlier in the tournament. Without waiting for an invitation, she declared her intention of coming in to finish her drinks.

It was quite possible that she had been sent to me by one of the opposing teams to prevent me from resting, so that I wouldn't play well the following day. On the other hand, if she had genuinely come seeking hospitality, it was my duty to show her some. I could have been selfish and gone back to sleep, or I could have sacrificed myself and shown her the traditional hospitality associated with the East.

Always a patriot, I won't tell you what path I chose — I will only tell you that kindness and decency have their own reward. The next day I played with added vigor, and we easily won both our matches. If the whole thing had been a Machiavellian plot by one of our opponents to spike me, it didn't work.

When the round-robin stage was over, we found that we had not only qualified but were lying second to America. This was beyond our wildest expectations. It was embarrassing only to Fazli, who had booked his return flight for the next day. He had to buy a new ticket!

In the semifinal, we played against Argentina, the South American champions, while the United States played Poland. With luck comes confidence, and when the semifinal started, our whole team was still playing in Heat #1, feeling unstoppable. My partner, Masood, is usually an intense and emotionless player, but even he found a smile when the opponents bid a grand slam when he was looking at the ace of trumps. This was the hand, North-South vulnerable:

North
♠ J
♡ A K J 10 9 8 5
◊ Q 8 6 4
♣ A

West (Masood)
♠ 10 6 3
♡ 7 4
◊ A 10 7
♣ Q 10 9 8 3

East (Zia)
♠ 9 7 5 2
♡ 6 3 2
◊ J
♣ K J 6 5 4

South
♠ A K Q 8 4
♡ Q
◊ K 9 5 3 2
♣ 7 2

	Masood		Zia
South	West	North	East
1 ♠	pass	2 ♡	pass
3 ◊	pass	4 ♣	double
4 ◊	pass	5 ♣	pass
5 ◊	pass	6 ◊	pass
pass	7 ♣	pass	pass
7 ◊	double	(all pass)	

If Masood hadn't sacrificed in seven clubs, it isn't clear what would have happened in six diamonds. In the other room, Nisar, in five diamonds, guessed the trumps correctly for plus 620. In our room, South guessed them also, but he was in seven doubled. One down gave us 200 and 13 imps.

One of my rubber-bridge tips came through at the right moment, on Board 9 of the semifinal, East-West vulnerable:

North (Masood)
♠ A K Q
♡ 10 6 5
♢ 7 5 2
♣ Q J 10 7

West
♠ 10 5 4
♡ 3 2
♢ K 10 4 3
♣ A K 9 3

East
♠ J 9 8 7 2
♡ A K 4
♢ Q J 8 6
♣ 6

South (Zia)
♠ 6 3
♡ Q J 9 8 7
♢ A 9
♣ 8 5 4 2

	Masood		Zia
West	North	East	South
—	1 NT (1)	pass	pass (2)
double (3)	pass	pass	2 ◊ (4)
double (5)	pass	pass	2 ♡ (6)
pass	pass	double (7)	(all pass)

(1) 12-14 points
(2) It's usually better to pass a weak notrump than to take out to two hearts when you cannot handle a two-spade bid by the opponents.
(3) frisky, to say the least
(4) I wanted to be doubled in two hearts, so I set the bait.
(5) West assumed that East had a good hand.
(6) closing in for the kill
(7) hooked

I had no trouble making two hearts doubled for plus 470.

These two hands were typical of the way things were going for us. We were sailing along — but suddenly there was a hiccup, or two hiccups to be exact.

The World Bridge Federation had recently started using screens for major events. The screen consists of a board with a small curtain in it placed diagonally across the table so that partners cannot see each other. Your bids are made by placing pieces of cardboard in a tray, which slides under the curtain during the auction. The purpose is to remove any accidental or intentional voice inflections. After the bidding, the curtain is raised so that the players can see the cards, but not one another's faces. The board runs under the table as well so that partners' feet may not touch.

Instances of cheating at the top level are few and far between, but when they do occur, they receive vast amounts of publicity, which is detrimental to the game as a whole. So the authorities try to ensure security in tournaments as best they can. Most of the top players prefer screens — I, for one, do not always have control of my reactions, which I must have when there are no screens around. By nature I am very demonstrative and emotional. I like the freedom of smiling or even grimacing at my partner while he is playing or bidding a hand. This is fine only if he can't see me, which is the case behind screens.

Not being able to hear your partner make his bid, as you've been used to all your life, can sometimes be confusing. With little experience at this level or practice with screens, it was not surprising that we had an accident or two. On two separate occasions one of our players mis-saw the bidding and ended up at a high level in the opponent's suit — going for big numbers.

But this was the only problem we had, and we ended up winning the semifinal in some comfort, while America won the other.

We were in the final of the world championships! Where were those who said we shouldn't be? Where were those who said Pakistan could only play physical sports like cricket, squash and hockey?

By now we were the Cinderella team, and the whole world loves an underdog. All the spectators were rooting for us. We were over the moon.

It was hard for us to buckle down to playing well in the final. We had already surpassed our own expectations. The Americans, on the other hand, had come expecting to reach this stage. They were mentally prepared for this moment; for them the battle was just starting.

Our best chance, perhaps our only chance, would be if we could score enough points to take a large lead while the American sponsor was playing. American teams are often made up of five full-time professionals and one sponsor who hires them. The sponsor is an enthusiast whose standard is usually below international level. To be called a World Champion though, each person had to play at least one-third of the deals.

Our free style and aggressive game was very effective in scoring heavily against weaker players, just as it could be inferior when faced with the methods of *better* players. We had been hoping that while the sponsor played his third of the match, we would have our one chance of really doing well. But an unexpected blow was waiting for us. For the first time in such a situation, the American team decided it was too dangerous to play their own sponsor against us, and they decided to sit him out for the whole final. The merits or demerits of this action were not our business. We did know it was a severe blow to our hopes of victory.

The final was 96 boards, and after 48 the score was: Pakistan 95, U.S.A. 92. It was halfway through the final and we were leading! Did we really have a chance? Sadly, now the tide turned, and as the miracle slipped away, we came quickly back to earth.

There are always regrets. There were many hands on which we could have played better. Masood and I were especially tired, having played almost 600 deals without a rest. But the hand that generated the most publicity was certainly this one.

Sitting West with neither side vulnerable, you pick up this hand:

♠ Q 9 8 7   ♡ A Q 9 6 4   ◊ 6   ♣ K 9 7

The auction proceeds as follows:

You			
West	North	East	South
1 ♡	3 ♡*	double	3 NT*
pass	pass	double*	pass
pass	redouble*	(all pass)	

3 ♡ = "Partner, I have a solid minor suit on the side; please bid three notrump if you have a heart stopper."

3 NT = "I have a heart stopper."

Double of 3 NT = "I don't think they can make this."

Redouble = expressing doubt: "I am worried about the whole affair. I have my solid suit, but nothing else."

As you think about your lead, I should tell you that your opponents are the famous pair, Jeff Meckstroth and Eric Rodwell, who, as usual, are involved in a potentially huge swing. Take your time; the fate of the World Championship may hinge on your lead.

What is your choice?

173

Leading a low heart is bad because North-South probably have seven diamond tricks, the ♡K and one black ace. In fact, on a heart lead, declarer would have made 10 tricks for plus 950 and 13 imps.

If you selected a spade, you would have been minus 750 and 12 imps.

Finally, if you picked a club, you would have been plus 2200 and 20 imps! The *defenders* can win the first 10 tricks!

Our player judged to lead a spade.

This was the full deal:

North
♠ 2
♡ 10 8
♢ A K Q 10 8 5 2
♣ 6 4 2

West
♠ Q 9 8 7
♡ A Q 9 6 4
♢ 6
♣ K 9 7

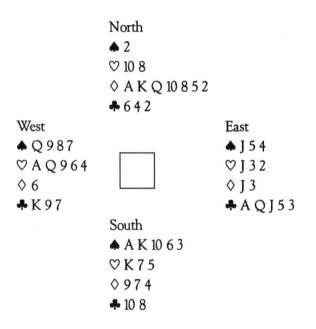

East
♠ J 5 4
♡ J 3 2
♢ J 3
♣ A Q J 5 3

South
♠ A K 10 6 3
♡ K 7 5
♢ 9 7 4
♣ 10 8

I could give you many arguments for and against the various leads, but I prefer not to talk about this hand any longer than necessary — it still hurts too much.

As the points slipped away steadily, and the dream with them, we didn't give up. But fighting from behind is not easy, and this often made matters even worse. However, there were some cheeky moments.

This was board 67:

South dealer
East-West vulnerable

```
                    North
                    ♠ 7 5 3 2
                    ♡ 7 4
                    ◊ A 7 4 2
                    ♣ A 7 6
West                                    East
♠ 10 8                                  ♠ Q 9 6
♡ A 9 6 2          ┌─────┐              ♡ K Q 10 8 3
◊ K 6 5            │     │              ◊ J 8 3
♣ Q J 5 2          └─────┘              ♣ 8 4
                    South (Zia)
                    ♠ A K J 4
                    ♡ J 5
                    ◊ Q 10 9
                    ♣ K 10 9 3
```

I was in one notrump — yes, I know two spades is a better contract, but that's one of the problems of playing weak notrumps. I received the ♣2 lead (6, 8, 10). I returned the ♣3, West put in the ♣J, and I won with dummy's ace.

Now I called for the ♡4 (3, J, 2)! Yes, a heart to the jack held!

This deceptive play often works, even against the best opposition, as you see here. It looks flamboyant, but requires no great level of ability. Whenever you're in a notrump contract and can see the defenders are about to switch to a suit you can't stand, try the effect of playing the suit before they do — it might mislead them. It is much better than giving up.

Sometimes this play can lead to unexpected benefits. Here is an example of Gabriel Chagas, the Brazilian star, in action.

South dealer
East-West vulnerable

North
♠ K 4
♡ K 5
♢ A K J 9 5 4
♣ 10 6 5

South (Chagas)
♠ A Q J 2
♡ A 7 6 3
♢ 8 7 2
♣ Q 4

Chagas

South	West	North	East
1 NT	pass	3 NT	(all pass)

West led the ♠6. Happy to have avoided a club lead, Chagas counted his top tricks and found eight: four spades, two hearts and two diamonds. If the diamonds were coming in, there was no problem — he didn't need four spade tricks. So he won the first trick with dummy's ♠K and dropped the ♠J from hand as a "just-in-case" play. He wasn't quite sure why, but it seemed like a good idea at the time.

However, when he cashed the ♢A, West discarded the ♠3.

If ever a contract looked hopeless, this was it. He invoked Rule #1: In such situations, play their suit before they do. Chagas called for the ♣5 and put up the ♣Q. West won with the ace, and didn't sneeringly shoot back a club. Instead he switched to a heart (to East's queen and South's ace).

Unfortunately, because of his deceptive play on the first trick, Chagas no longer even had the eight tricks he started with. But, hoping to induce a second spade discard from West, he led another diamond toward the dummy. West obliged by discarding a spade, giving the spade trick back. It was a lot of work to break even.

Not yet willing to give up by cashing his eight tricks, and thinking that it was worth the investment to risk down two, Chagas ducked the diamond to East's 10.

He was still alive when East returned a heart to the king. This was the end-position:

North
♠ 4
♡ —
◇ K J 5 4
♣ 10 6

☐

South (Chagas)
♠ A Q 2
♡ 7 6
◇ 8
♣ 4

Chagas cashed his three spade tricks. West threw a heart on the third spade and East, in obvious discomfort, pitched the ♣8 and ♣J. Now Chagas exited with a heart. West won with the ♡J and led a club to his partner's bare ♣K. East was endplayed, forced to lead into dummy's ◇K-J.

Chagas was plus 600 — Brazilian magic at its best. This was the full hand:

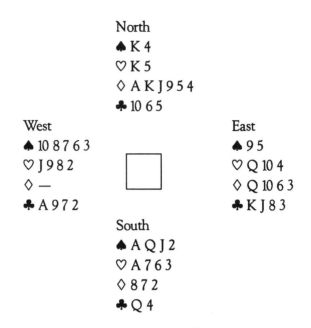

North
♠ K 4
♡ K 5
♢ A K J 9 5 4
♣ 10 6 5

West
♠ 10 8 7 6 3
♡ J 9 8 2
♢ —
♣ A 9 7 2

East
♠ 9 5
♡ Q 10 4
♢ Q 10 6 3
♣ K J 8 3

South
♠ A Q J 2
♡ A 7 6 3
♢ 8 7 2
♣ Q 4

Even the best players can be fooled by this bold deceptive play. If you twisted my arm, I could probably recall a hand recorded live for British television a few years ago in which Rob Sheehan, the English internationalist, made almost an identical play against me. Rather embarrassingly, I ducked, much to the amusement of a couple of million viewers.

As time ran out in Rye, we did have a few defiant moments. Masood had played to the point of exhaustion, and now, beaten but not bowed, this hand, board 92, was a fitting tribute to his efforts:

East dealer
North-South vulnerable

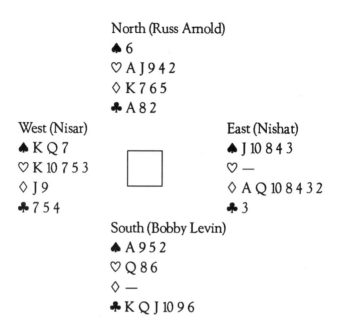

North (Russ Arnold)
♠ 6
♡ A J 9 4 2
◊ K 7 6 5
♣ A 8 2

West (Nisar)
♠ K Q 7
♡ K 10 7 5 3
◊ J 9
♣ 7 5 4

East (Nishat)
♠ J 10 8 4 3
♡ —
◊ A Q 10 8 4 3 2
♣ 3

South (Bobby Levin)
♠ A 9 5 2
♡ Q 8 6
◊ —
♣ K Q J 10 9 6

This is what happened in the Closed Room:

Nisar	Arnold	Nishat	Levin
West	North	East	South
—	—	pass	1 ♣
1 ♡	2 ◊	pass	2 ♠
pass	2 NT	pass	3 ♣
pass	3 NT	(all pass)	

Nishat (East) led the ♠3 (ace, king, 6). Declarer led the
♡Q, covered by the king and ace. Now with the marked
finesse of the ♡9, Arnold had 10 top tricks.

The action in the Open Room was more exciting:

179

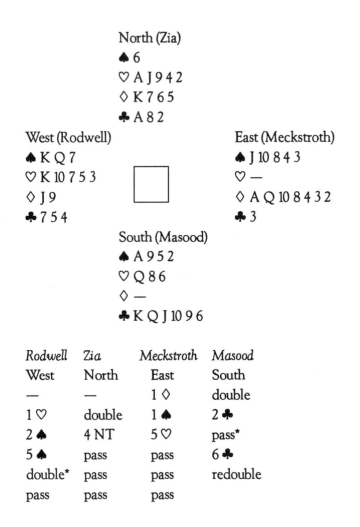

North (Zia)
♠ 6
♡ A J 9 4 2
◊ K 7 6 5
♣ A 8 2

West (Rodwell)
♠ K Q 7
♡ K 10 7 5 3
◊ J 9
♣ 7 5 4

East (Meckstroth)
♠ J 10 8 4 3
♡ —
◊ A Q 10 8 4 3 2
♣ 3

South (Masood)
♠ A 9 5 2
♡ Q 8 6
◊ —
♣ K Q J 10 9 6

Rodwell	Zia	Meckstroth	Masood
West	North	East	South
—	—	1 ◊	double
1 ♡	double	1 ♠	2 ♣
2 ♠	4 NT	5 ♡	pass*
5 ♠	pass	pass	6 ♣
double*	pass	pass	redouble
pass	pass	pass	

pass of 5 ♡ = systemically showing one ace
double of 6 ♣ = knowing his partner is ruffing hearts

Meckstroth and Rodwell play Precision, but the one-diamond opening bid was light even by their standards. Rodwell's one-heart bid was natural and forcing for one round, and my double was for penalties.

By the time Rodwell bid two spades, I knew what was happening and tried to clarify matters for Masood by using Blackwood.

Now Meckstroth — bidding for a third time on his seven points! — made an expert call, pinpointing the lead.

Finally, Masood did brilliantly, bidding six clubs and redoubling. They might have been about to win the Bermuda Bowl, but he made sure they remembered we were there.

The play was short. The ♡3 opening lead (an upside-down suit-preference for spades!) was ruffed by East, and back came the ♠J, won with the ace. Masood ruffed a spade, led back to the ♣K, then led the ♡Q, covered by the king and ace. He ruffed a diamond, ruffed a spade, ruffed a diamond, drew the last trump, finessed the ♡9, and had 12 tricks by way of one spade, three hearts, two spade ruffs in the dummy and six trumps in hand. We scored +1780 and 15 imps.

Despite losing the final we were not unhappy. The better team had won, which is as it should be, and we had vindicated our place in the tournament. Our players had done us proud, each one had played his heart out, and we could go home proudly with our silver medals. We hardly noticed that the medals proved to be more symbolic than real, being wooden cigarette boxes! Most of the team gave theirs to our delighted supporter, Beroze, who was crying with joy.

Among the lessons I learned from the invaluable experience of this tournament were the following:

1. Team spirit is as important as ability. There were at least two teams that lost bushels of points because of the unfriendly attitudes of their members. Our strengths were friendship and camaraderie.

2. Never discuss a hand at the table — never.

3. There are very few people who can have a disaster and suffer no adverse reaction, so whenever you have a disaster on a hand, regroup. By that I mean make a conscious effort to come to the next hand with a fresh mind. It is easy to be so caught up in a disaster without realizing that it affects you

for several ensuing deals. If it helps, get up and drink a glass of iced water, or go to the washroom, or walk around the room. Do anything, but snap out of it or you're dead.

4. Partners and teams should meet daily after the game to go over all the hands of interest, especially those where partnerships had a problem. Everybody does have accidents; it's no big deal, but it's vital to clear the air and get out the negative feelings from your system, rather than holding them in, feeling hurt or bitter. If at these sessions you feel your partner, yourself or a teammate went crazy, say so. I recommend an open discussion so that it becomes less personal and more fun.

We all commit idiocies from time to time; if you can accept that and laugh at them, you are heading in the right direction.

5. Understand the theory of the Three Heats and apply it.

6. Bridge is unlike any other game. No team is so much better that the underdog doesn't have a chance.

7. Never give up, and remember above all that the real tournament only begins at the final, no matter how much it seems you have achieved before.

11

New York, New York

The 1980s and 1990s

On the way back from Rye, I stopped in New York. Everything you hear about the city is true — you either love it or hate it.

The first night I was there, a taxi-driver told me that I looked like a waiter for wearing a dinner jacket, and a 60-year-old woman in the hotel bar offered to take me dancing at Regines discotheque. The second night I was there, the 60-year old woman told me I looked like a waiter, and the tax-driver offered to take me dancing!

By the third night, I'd had enough. I stayed home and left the two of them to go out together. My kind of town. I loved it instantly.

New York is where the action is. First there is rubber bridge at the Cavendish Club, the Regency and Al Roth's famous Mayfair Club, where the stakes range from low to astronomical, and where the players range from unbelievably bad to unbelievably good. Next there are the high-stake imp games (duplicate bridge) at the Mayfair and Cavendish. You draw for partners and teammates, and play eight-board matches. They are great fun and great practice, too.

American and British bridge clubs are quite different. In New York rubber-bridge games, you can play as many systems as you like. In Britain, some say that even Stayman and Blackwood should be banned. Reactions to errors have slightly different flavors, too. In New York, you are more likely to hear someone called by the endearing Americanism, "You moron!" than the more British reprimand, "Nasty setback, partner."

This was my first visit to the Cavendish, famous for its annual auction tournament, where the pairs are sold to bidders. I naturally came to play, but on the first occasion I watched. Kibitzing can be boring, unless someone of the caliber of Broadway Billy Eisenberg is playing the hand. I'm not easily impressed, but he managed it. Billy was once World Champion at bridge and backgammon at the same time. He also has the doubtful distinction of having resigned from the famous Aces team. They didn't allow enough late nights in a week to suit him. (He likes the fast lane.)

West dealer
None vulnerable

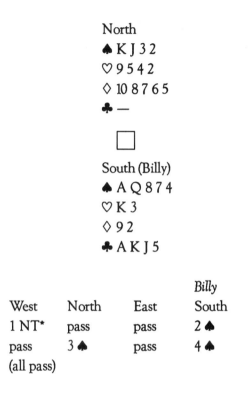

North
♠ K J 3 2
♡ 9 5 4 2
♢ 10 8 7 6 5
♣ —

South (Billy)
♠ A Q 8 7 4
♡ K 3
♢ 9 2
♣ A K J 5

			Billy
West	North	East	South
1 NT*	pass	pass	2 ♠
pass	3 ♠	pass	4 ♠
(all pass)			

1 NT = 15-17 points

West leads the ♠10. How would you play?

You have 21 points between you and dummy, which gives East a maximum of four points. You work out that West must have the ♡A, because if East had it, West would have led a top diamond from his honors. There's obviously no genuine chance to make the hand, unless you try the "Chinese finesse" (a finesse that can never work if the opponent covers your card; e.g., a phony finesse with A-2 opposite Q-3, in which you run the queen and it holds). That's what Eisenberg did. He won the opening lead with the ♠Q, and at trick two ran the ♣J, throwing a heart from the dummy!

Then he discarded two more heart losers on the ♣A-K. This was the full deal:

North
♠ K J 3 2
♡ 9 5 4 2
♢ 10 8 7 6 5
♣ —

West
♠ 10 9
♡ A Q J
♢ A Q 4 3
♣ Q 8 6 3

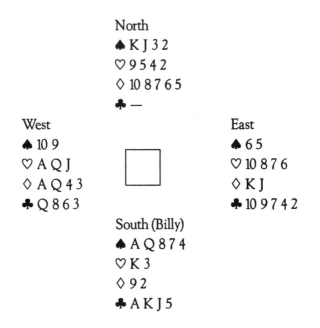

East
♠ 6 5
♡ 10 8 7 6
♢ K J
♣ 10 9 7 4 2

South (Billy)
♠ A Q 8 7 4
♡ K 3
♢ 9 2
♣ A K J 5

Would you have covered the ♣J?

The Chinese finesse works quite often. Officially it's a no-play play, but it comes up more often than you might imagine.

Desperate bidders need desperate plays. Take a look at this:

West dealer
East-West vulnerable

              North
              ♠ A 5 3
              ♡ 6 4
              ◊ A J 2
              ♣ Q 8 6 5 4
West   East
♠ Q 8 2   ♠ 10 9 4
♡ A K 2   ♡ Q J 8 7 3
◊ Q 9 7 5 4   ◊ 8 3
♣ J 2   ♣ A 10 9
              South (You)
              ♠ K J 7 6
              ♡ 10 9 5
              ◊ K 10 6
              ♣ K 7 3

                              You
West   North   East   South
1 ◊   pass   1 ♡   pass
2 ♡   pass   pass   2 ♠
pass   pass   3 ♡   pass
pass   3 ♠   (all pass)

True, you have pushed them one too high, but your partner couldn't leave well enough alone. However, maybe you can make three spades.

West leads the ♡A (4, Q, 5). He cashes the ♡K (6, 3, 10), then switches to the ♣J (4, 10, K). How do you continue?

With two hearts already lost and two clubs still to lose, you need to make four spade tricks. For a start, they must break 3-3. But from his opening bid and the play so far, West is marked with the queen. The only chance is to play as if you have the ♠10. Lead the ♠J from hand and hope West doesn't cover.

If he doesn't cover, ruff your heart loser in the dummy, cash the ♠A, play a diamond to the king, draw trumps and take the diamond finesse.

I had intended to stay in New York one week. I was still there a month later. During my visit, I discovered that the top Americans had thought deeply about parts of the game that hadn't even been considered by most of the world.

Take this hand. You, West, hold:

♠ A 7 4 3   ♡ A 7 4 3   ♢ 10 8 2   ♣ 7 6

The bidding is short: South opens five clubs and everybody passes. You've read your text-books, so you lead the ♠A. After the dummy is tabled, this is what you see:

North
♠ Q 6 5
♡ Q 6 5
♢ A K Q J 5
♣ 8 2

West (You)
♠ A 7 4 3
♡ A 7 4 3
♢ 10 8 2
♣ 7 6

On your ♠A, partner plays an encouraging ♠8. You're a careful player, so you cash the ♡A. Partner plays the ♡9. Well, well, he's got both kings. Which one do you attempt to cash?

If you gave this problem to 99 percent of the world, they would all reply with learned and doubtful logic. The truth is that they wouldn't have a clue. If you had ever met "The Beast," it would be easy. The Beast — alias Ira Rubin — has a simple rule: In cash-out situations, a high odd card shows encouragement with an odd number in the suit and a high even card shows an original even number. Simple yet effective. So in the above example the ♠8 would show four spades, and the ♡9 five hearts. You should lead to your partner's ♠K.

The full hand was:

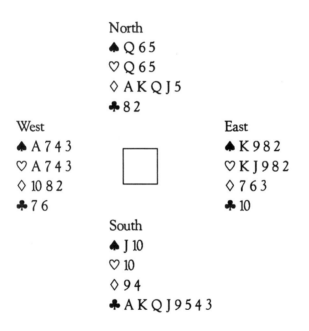

North
♠ Q 6 5
♡ Q 6 5
♢ A K Q J 5
♣ 8 2

West
♠ A 7 4 3
♡ A 7 4 3
♢ 10 8 2
♣ 7 6

East
♠ K 9 8 2
♡ K J 9 8 2
♢ 7 6 3
♣ 10

South
♠ J 10
♡ 10
♢ 9 4
♣ A K Q J 9 5 4 3

The same principle can apply when you've overcalled in a suit. Partner leads a high card, say the ace or king, and you can signal encouragement as well as give count at the same time. If partner doesn't have the appropriate odd or even card, you won't be worse off than you were before.

Rubin was one of the regulars at the Cavendish. He was nicknamed The Beast for his monstrous behavior and his verbal attacks on everybody — partners and opponents alike. He's 6' 4" tall and gargles razor blades for breakfast. He has lived up to his reputation many times.

One famous incident occurred when he was playing with Matt Granovetter. Matt forgot to split his honors, letting an impossible contract make. Anticipating Rubin's wrath, he ran to the men's bathroom, hoping to find shelter in a well-bolted cubicle. Nothing is safe from The Beast. Rubin not only followed him there, he even pounding the cubicle door in an insane rage to continue the attack at closer quarters.

Rubin was impossible to play with or against, but like so many of the inhabitants of the bridge world, he veers between genius and monster. I've learned a lot from him in his more human moments. He is an encyclopaedia of useful bridge information.

First, try this hand. You're West:

```
                         North
                         ♠ K Q 5 4
                         ♡ Q 9
                         ◊ K J 9 3
                         ♣ J 10 7
         West (You)
         ♠ A 3
         ♡ K 8 7 2        ┌──────┐
         ◊ 8 4 2          │      │
         ♣ K 9 8 6        └──────┘
```

South	West	North	East
1 ♣	pass	1 ◊	pass
1 ♠	pass	4 ♠	(all pass)

You open with the ♠A. What do you lead at trick two?

Most people would answer, "It's a guess."

Rubin proposed an easy solution: suit preference in the trump suit. On this hand partner would play the ♠J under the ace, asking for a heart switch.

The full deal:

```
                 North
                 ♠ K Q 5 4
                 ♡ Q 9
                 ◊ K J 9 3
                 ♣ J 10 7
 West                              East
 ♠ A 3                             ♠ J 8 2
 ♡ K 8 7 2           ┌───┐         ♡ A 10 4 3
 ◊ 8 4 2            │   │         ◊ 10 7 6 5
 ♣ K 9 8 6           └───┘         ♣ 5 2
                 South
                 ♠ 10 9 7 6
                 ♡ J 6 5
                 ◊ A Q
                 ♣ A Q 4 3
```

By the time I was ready to leave New York, two things were clear: There were more good players in America than anywhere else. And, if I wanted to compete with the best, I had to start spending time there.

So I added the States to my growing list of homes. I hopped from one country to another, running through passports like packs of cards. It was a strange feeling when someone asked me, "Where do you live?" I had to reply, "I don't know." But that was the truth.

Although traveling may sound glamorous, it wasn't. I was motivated neither by the lure of making money (most tournaments are strictly amateur) nor by the celebrity status of a bridge player (there isn't any).

Cricketers and footballers might need a bodyguard to

keep girls out of their rooms; bridge players need one to bring them in. As for the celebrity idea — to the public, even the better-known bridge players are usually no more than names in a newspaper column. I remember visiting a club in the Middle East where, before I could introduce myself, one of the players asked me if I knew his good friend Zia Mahmood!

On the other hand, to find something that you really enjoy is a bonus not to be taken lightly. While most people dream about retiring and wandering around the world to follow their passions, I was already doing just that. As George Raft once said: "Part of my money went on gambling, part went on horses, part went on women — and the rest I spent foolishly."

And I have loved every moment.

Wall Street is packed with good bridge players, none better known than Alan "Ace" Greenberg and Jimmy Cayne, Chairman and President of Bear Stearns. On one visit to New York, I joined their regular team (including Jimmy "Sparky" Rosenbloom, Matt Granovetter and his charming and talented wife Pamela) to play in the prestigious Reisinger event. We ended up winning — that was the good news. A lucky hand turned out to be even better news. Sitting West, you hold:

♠ 9 7 4 3　♡ 6 2　◇ 5 4　♣ Q 10 8 4 2

	You		
South	West	North	East
1 ♣	pass	1 ♡	pass
1 NT*	pass	3 ♡*	pass
3 NT	(all pass)		

1 NT = 15-17 points
3 ♡ = forcing.

What is your lead?

Have a look at the whole hand before deciding.

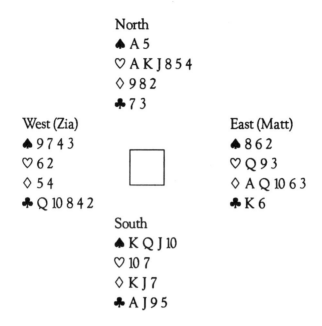

North
♠ A 5
♡ A K J 8 5 4
◊ 9 8 2
♣ 7 3

West (Zia)
♠ 9 7 4 3
♡ 6 2
◊ 5 4
♣ Q 10 8 4 2

East (Matt)
♠ 8 6 2
♡ Q 9 3
◊ A Q 10 6 3
♣ K 6

South
♠ K Q J 10
♡ 10 7
◊ K J 7
♣ A J 9 5

The contract looks impregnable. Clutching at straws, instead of the conventional standard lead such as fourth best in spades, I led the *four* of diamonds! Look what happened. My partner, Matt, liked the lead. Playing his part, he won with the ◊ A and returned the ◊ 3, in theory showing that he had started with four diamonds.

The declarer was worried that if he finessed the ◊ J, I might win with the queen and switch to a club. So he logically won with the ◊ K. After all, he was safe on any distribution except East's having five diamonds, which was "impossible" on the play.

Declarer took the heart finesse — and almost fell off his chair when Matt won with the ♡ Q and cashed *three* diamond tricks.

Why this strange opening lead? First, I have a theory that it's correct to try something unusual in a desperate situation.

This hand fit nicely — our prospects looked hopeless. Second, South was known to have at least four clubs, because he denied three hearts when he bid three notrump. So a club lead was out; anyway, I hate leading the opponents' suit. Third, partner couldn't have good spades, because he didn't overcall one spade. And fourth, he may hold good diamonds without the values for a two-level intervention. The "normal" lead is the ♢5, but with such a terrible hand, I thought I might as well try the effect of a falsecard: the ♢4. Who knows, maybe something good would happen.

It did. The declarer went down; and "Ace" and Jimmy enjoyed the lead so much that they invited me into the most exclusive club in the world, the Regency Whist Club on East 67th and 5th Avenue.

The Regency

"Rockefeller hasn't got any money."

"What do you mean, he's worth over 50 million."

"That's just what I mean, he hasn't got any money."

If you had happened to overhear the conversation in one of the plush rooms of the Regency Whist Club, you wouldn't have been too surprised. There are people who have money, and there are people who are *rich*.

Most bridge games have a few interesting people; this one had nothing but. With regulars like the Nose, the Fox and the Weasel, you might mistakenly think that you were dealing with a strange group. In fact, the game boasted some of the most powerful men in America — and some of the most generous.

Take Milton.

Milton Petrie is in his 80s. He loves bridge with a passion, plays daily and is always the first to arrive at the club. Well known for his wealth, he is even better known for his philanthropy. When he is cut out of the rubber, he scours newspapers, picking out deserving cases to give a helping hand to. He hands out money to worthwhile causes as if it's going out of style. Most of his donations are made anonymously, but I heard about one six-figure contribution that he made to an orphanage. When the grateful beneficiaries turned up at his office to thank him, Petrie doubled the donation.

If a policeman or fireman is killed in the line of duty, his family could well have a trust fund set up to help them — courtesy of Petrie. He enjoys his daily "fix" of bridge, but avoids unnecessary conversation. In fact, I had been playing at the club for two days before he said a word to me. Then I almost wished it had stayed that way. The contract was three notrump, and dummy had no side entry. This was the diamond suit:

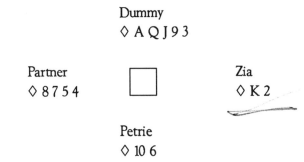

Dummy
◊ A Q J 9 3

Partner   Zia
◊ 8 7 5 4   ◊ K 2

Petrie
◊ 10 6

When Petrie ran the ◊ 10, I ducked my king. When he didn't guess what I had done, he finessed again, going down when he would have made the contract if I had won the first diamond trick.

When he saw what I had done, he first growled, "You son of a bitch." Then he smiled and added, "Nice play."

Jack Dreyfus, founder of the Dreyfus Mutual Fund, is another committed bridge lover. Successful in everything he's tried (golf, tennis, even gin rummy), he's also had his share of luck. Years ago he was confident that 3-D pictures would be the thing of the future. He put most of his money into Polaroid shares. 3-D was a disaster, but the company invented a new camera. The stock soared and Dreyfus used his 3-D glasses to count the fortune he made. Now retired, Dreyfus has devoted his time and wealth to his charitable medical foundation. He's also famous for somehow always dealing himself the ♠A, but he may well make the Guinness Book of Records for having put down the best dummy in history — this one:

♠ A ♡ A K J 10 9 8 7 6 3 2 ◊ A ♣ 4

The story is easier to understand if you hear that his partner was the lovable, but on occasion disaster-prone, "Fox."

Dreyfus dealt and opened two clubs.

The Fox bid the negative two diamonds.

Dreyfus's right-hand opponent leaped to five clubs.

Dreyfus "closed" the auction with a bid of six hearts.

Well, almost closed.

He hadn't got past the Fox, who still had to show his ♠ Q J 9 8 7 6 3.

"Six spades!" he offered.

Dreyfus gave up. Seven hearts had no chance, and who knew what spades the Fox held? Not enough.

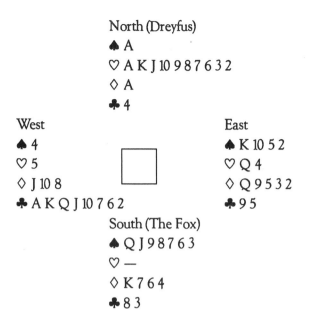

North (Dreyfus)
♠ A
♡ A K J 10 9 8 7 6 3 2
◊ A
♣ 4

West
♠ 4
♡ 5
◊ J 10 8
♣ A K Q J 10 7 6 2

East
♠ K 10 5 2
♡ Q 4
◊ Q 9 5 3 2
♣ 9 5

South (The Fox)
♠ Q J 9 8 7 6 3
♡ —
◊ K 7 6 4
♣ 8 3

One of the calmest people in the world, Dreyfus didn't say a word as the Fox went three down. But when the Fox said, "Couldn't you rebid your hearts once?" Jack finally exploded.

However, you can't stay mad at The Fox for long. He has a habit of coming up with one of his original remarks that is sure to make you laugh. Once when he seemed totally unsurprised that our hopeless contract had made, I asked him if he realized how lucky we had been. "Oh yes, of course I knew. But I'm Jewish and miracles are quite common in our religion." What else could a simple Pakistani say but "Oi vay!"

Sam Stayman is another regular at the Regency. His name must be the best known in the whole bridge world. Now in his 80s, he still plays as well as he did when winning three world titles in the 1950s. Alan Sontag, in his book, *The Bridge Bum*, relates a story about someone who was invited to Stayman's Park Avenue apartment. Almost immediately, the visitor gasped, "This must cost you a fortune." "No," Stayman replied, "it costs me nothing. I own the whole block."

North
♠ A 7
♡ Q 8 4
♢ A Q 2
♣ A Q 10 9 3

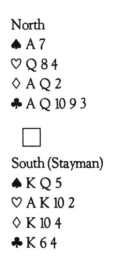

South (Stayman)
♠ K Q 5
♡ A K 10 2
♢ K 10 4
♣ K 6 4

South	West	North	East
1 NT	pass	4 ♣*	pass
4 ♡*	pass	5 ♣*	pass
5 ♢*	pass	7 NT	(all pass)

4 ♣ = Gerber, asking for aces
4 ♡ = one ace
5 ♣ = Gerber, asking for kings
5 ♢ = four kings

West led the ♠J. What is your line of play?

It looks so easy — which is the time when an expert becomes doubly careful. Stayman seemed to have 14 top tricks: three spades, three hearts, three diamonds and five clubs. The only problem would be if the clubs broke badly. The real expert postpones the moment of truth.

Stayman cashed the ♣A, just to check that they weren't 5-0. Then he took his major-suit winners, discarding a club from dummy on the third spade. East pitched low diamonds on both the third spade and third heart. Finally, Stayman cashed the ♢K and led a diamond to the ace, all following.

He paused to count. West was known to have started with six spades, four hearts, two diamonds and one club. East had to have begun with four clubs. Stayman called for the ♣10 and ran it. He led a club to the king, a diamond to the queen, and cashed the ♣Q for his contract.

Corporate Challenge

You are never too young or too old to start playing duplicate. Last year Petrie and Dreyfus took the plunge when they joined a team representing Corporate America. They played a match against the British Parliamentary team. Their team was impressive. Captained by Larry Tisch, Chairman of CBS television, it included names whose very mention could affect the Dow Jones index: Jimmy Cayne, Ace Greenberg, Milton Petrie, George Gillespie III, Warren Buffett and Malcolm Forbes. No less impressive were their opponents: the Duke of Atholl, Lord Lever and several MPs. They were captained by Sir Peter Emery. Also playing was Lord Smith, a famous surgeon who was equally famous in the bridge world for once removing 34 gallstones from the English bridge player Maurice Harrison-Gray, with the statement, "Enough for a small slam in notrumps."

The match was held in Malcolm Forbes's Battersea home. I was lucky to be asked to act as an MC — lucky because it gave me an opportunity to see Forbes's house. What a house! A journey into a private world of treasures that outshone any museum. Every inch of the walls was smothered by his unique collection of Victorian art. The corridors were packed to overflowing with priceless antiques. Fabergé eggs were casually spread around like shells on a beach.

Forbes, who once openly declared that bridge was much more fascinating than making money, spent the day alternately charming the players and playing in the match. He certainly knew his way around the card table. Here is a hand that he played with Tisch:

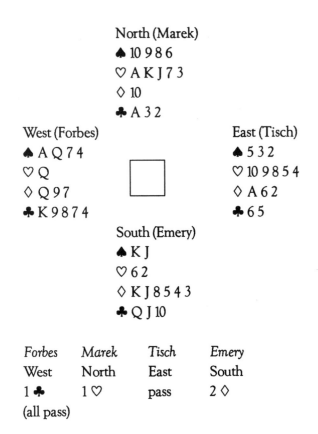

North (Marek)
♠ 10 9 8 6
♡ A K J 7 3
♢ 10
♣ A 3 2

West (Forbes)
♠ A Q 7 4
♡ Q
♢ Q 9 7
♣ K 9 8 7 4

East (Tisch)
♠ 5 3 2
♡ 10 9 8 5 4
♢ A 6 2
♣ 6 5

South (Emery)
♠ K J
♡ 6 2
♢ K J 8 5 4 3
♣ Q J 10

Forbes	Marek	Tisch	Emery
West	North	East	South
1 ♣	1 ♡	pass	2 ♢
(all pass)			

Forbes led the ♡Q. Emery won in the dummy, then ran the ♢10, losing to West's queen. Now Forbes made a tricky play, switching to the *nine* of clubs. However, declarer wasn't fooled, running it to his queen. Next came the ♢K to East's ace. Tisch could have given his partner a heart ruff, but he could see that it would be the effective end of the defense. Instead, he made the excellent play of returning his second club, Forbes playing the ♣K to lock declarer in dummy.

Now the defenders had to collect two spades, two diamonds, a heart ruff and a club ruff for one down.

The American team narrowly lost the match, but the following day they lost much more. After returning to his New Jersey home, Malcolm Forbes, a man who had a life-long love affair with life, died of a heart attack.

12

Luck be a Lady

Atlantic City, the Final

Walking into the playing area just before one o'clock, I noticed that it appeared larger than the previous day. This was because most of the tables had been removed, leaving only 10: all that was needed for the 40 remaining players. For the first time the atmosphere seemed charged, the smiles of yesterday looked less warm, and the competitors glanced warily at each other, sizing up the opposition. With the field reduced, the enemy was now more visible, more real. There were no soft touches left. The next two days would be tough.

The spectators seemed to sense the tension, too. There were more of them, and they spoke quietly, even solemnly. There were even a couple of newspaper reporters, something that is almost unheard of at a bridge event. I hoped I would give them a story. My first partner was already at the table.

"Everything natural, if you don't mind. I play no conventions."

I was slightly surprised by this admission, but it was fine by me. We would only play two boards together, and 99 percent of the time system would make no difference anyway. Conventions come up less than people realize.

But today was in the one-percent bracket. I picked up:

♠ 10 7 6 ♡ 5 ◇ A Q 10 ♣ Q J 10 9 8 5

Partner		Zia	
South	West	North	East
2 ♠	pass	3 ♣	pass
3 ♡	pass	3 ♠	pass
4 ♠	pass	6 ♠	(all pass)

My choices over four spades were restricted because we weren't using Blackwood. I could pass (exceedingly cautious) or bid five spades (a slight underbid) or jump to six spades (a gross overbid). Naturally I chose the overbid — what the heck, it was the first board.

West led the ◇3, and this was what my partner could see:

North
♠ 10 7 6
♡ 5
◇ A Q 10
♣ Q J 10 9 8 5

☐

South
♠ A K Q J 9
♡ K Q J 7 2
◇ 5 2
♣ K

How would you play the hand?

In the embarrassing position of having two aces out, it's right to finesse the ♢10, hoping to get rid of the club loser.

My partner coolly finessed the *queen* of diamonds, then played a club to his king and West's ace. Luckily West continued with another diamond. Now my partner drew trumps in three rounds, ending in the dummy, and discarded all five heart losers on my club winners. Plus 980!

This was the full deal:

North
♠ 10 7 6
♡ 5
♢ A Q 10
♣ Q J 10 9 8 5

West
♠ 5 2
♡ 9 6 4
♢ K J 6 3
♣ A 7 3 2

East
♠ 8 4 3
♡ A 10 8 3
♢ 9 8 7 4
♣ 6 4

South
♠ A K Q J 9
♡ K Q J 7 2
♢ 5 2
♣ K

A triumph for no conventions! When did a Blackwood player last bid and make a slam with two aces out? This was better than roulette.

Talking about two aces out, try this lead problem. You're West, holding:

♠ 4 ♡ A K J 10 6 5 ◇ 10 7 2 ♣ A Q 9

The auction proceeds along an unusual path:

	You		
South	West	North	East
3 ♠	4 ♡	7 ♠	(all pass)

Well, what is your lead?
After you decide, look at the whole hand.

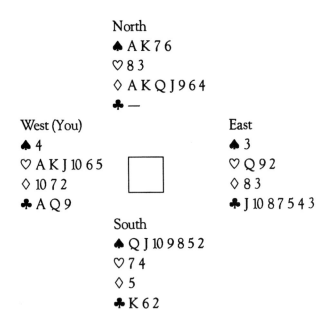

North
♠ A K 7 6
♡ 8 3
◇ A K Q J 9 6 4
♣ —

West (You)
♠ 4
♡ A K J 10 6 5
◇ 10 7 2
♣ A Q 9

East
♠ 3
♡ Q 9 2
◇ 8 3
♣ J 10 8 7 5 4 3

South
♠ Q J 10 9 8 5 2
♡ 7 4
◇ 5
♣ K 6 2

Nice bid, North! You didn't forget to ask who was sitting North, did you? Well, who he was doesn't matter as much as knowing what *type* of player he was. Against a tricky North, lead the ♡A or ♡K. Against a less tricky one, the ♣A is more likely to be right.

At the time, West led the ♣A. Minus 2210.

I don't mind admitting that at times I've been lucky in cards — sometimes enormously so. Some years ago, four of us, on board the boat *The Canberra*, were being filmed by the BBC for a TV series. We played Chicago-style rubber bridge for seven days for a nominal stake. At the end of the trip, the winner received a £10,000 prize.

As we entered the last deal of the final rubber, the Canadian, Sami Kehela, was leading, and I was second, 800 points behind. It didn't look good for me.

There were three passes to me and I held:

♠ A J 10 7 ♡ K 10 6 ◊ J 2 ♣ A K 10 9

I passed!

A Chicago stanza is only completed once all four hands are played. If a hand is passed out, it is redealt. Needing 800 points, I had to bid a slam or get an unlikely penalty. It was improbable that with only 16 points I could make a slam opposite a passed partner. Maybe my next hand would be better.

Actually I had already been lucky. Kehela, holding two aces, might have opened in first seat. He knew I needed a slam to win, and because he was holding two aces himself, I couldn't make one.

This was the new deal:

East dealer
All vulnerable

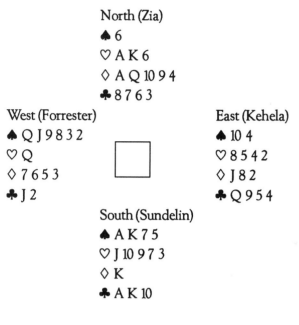

North (Zia)
♠ 6
♡ A K 6
◇ A Q 10 9 4
♣ 8 7 6 3

West (Forrester)
♠ Q J 9 8 3 2
♡ Q
◇ 7 6 5 3
♣ J 2

East (Kehela)
♠ 10 4
♡ 8 5 4 2
◇ J 8 2
♣ Q 9 5 4

South (Sundelin)
♠ A K 7 5
♡ J 10 9 7 3
◇ K
♣ A K 10

Forrester	Zia	Kehela	Sundelin
West	North	East	South
—	—	pass	1 ♡
pass	2 ◇	pass	2 ♠
pass	3 ♡	pass	4 ♣
pass	6 ♡	(all pass)	

My partner, P. O. Sundelin, a top Swedish internationalist, and I bid and made six hearts for +1430. I had won the competition by 6 rubber-bridge points.

Yes, I have been lucky.

Good first boards are lucky for me, or maybe it's easier to play confidently with a good result behind you. Whatever the reasons, I felt things were going well. They were.

At the end of the first final session in Atlantic City, I found I was sharing the lead with that very same P. O. Sundelin. The pack was bunched close behind — but at least it was behind. They would have to wait until tomorrow.

Today Lady Luck belonged to me.

* * * * * * * * *

That Old Black Magic

Voodoo, witch doctors, spells and lucky potions — gamblers have running love affairs with Lady Luck, and bridge players will try anything once to improve their fortune.

You're not like that? Wanna bet? When was the last time you said, "Let's get out of these seats, they're unlucky." Or, "Give me the blues, the blues never lose."

These sayings go on and on. But how much of a part does luck really play in bridge? It's a tough question to answer. If we all lived for ever, probability states that everybody would have the same amount of luck. In the short run, some people are bound to be luckier than others.

Bridge players are always moaning about their bad luck. I've heard countless stories about losing streaks, but even the worst of them dries up sooner or later. And anyone on a permanent losing run has more to worry about than just bad luck. Remember, the odds never lie, and a good player will always win in the long run, just like a casino.

Superstition — now that's another matter altogether. People who play cards are invariably superstitious. Some think clothes hold the answer. They say a lady is one who never shows her underwear unintentionally, but Nicola Gardener-Smith, an English women's world champion, has a preference for her lucky tartan underwear when she's playing in an important tournament. Whatever turns you on!

Others stick to less personal items. Both Rixi Markus and Giorgio Belladonna are sure that pens have magical qualities. They keep switching them in synchronization with the ebb and flow of their sessions. They've won so much that maybe they know something.

Some think that transport is the answer. Brian Glubok, an American expert, believes that it's lucky to cycle to tournaments. Great — if you ever get there.

Others look to the heavens. A famous Italian player "moons" to the moon every New Year's Eve.

These and countless others are all possible, but I have my own way of escaping when things become desperate. Not long ago, a never-ending stream of losing confirmed my suspicions that the gods had finally deserted me. Things were so bad that there even had been times when I actually thought of going back to work for a living. I badly needed a sign, a zinger, that would lift me up and put me back on the path of my winning ways of the past. I found one on Madison Avenue and 56th Street: a vision.

She hypnotized me and then she was gone. A voice, a destiny, lady luck — who knows? — issued me with a challenge: "Get her to have a drink with you and your run of luck will change." What could I lose? I followed after her but she had disappeared. Frustrated, I got into the nearest cab. But luck was still playing her games, and as the cab started to move away from the curb, I spotted her again. She saw me, smiled and waved. It took me 10 seconds to get over the shock, two seconds to yell, "Stop!" to the cab driver and throw some money at him, and about 20 seconds to run back along Madison Avenue to find her.

"I'm a gambler who's going through a terrible run of bad luck. I am extremely superstitious and I know that if you walk the ten blocks with me to my club, it's going to break the bad run that I've been having."

Before she could reply, we started walking. If I were hypnotized before, now I was bewitched. Ten blocks later I had totally fallen for her.

"For the next three days I will go to the Mayfair Regent Hotel at six-thirty. I'll drink one glass of champagne and leave. If you'd like to see me again, come there. If not, it was a pleasure meeting you."

What else could I say? She smiled, shook my hand and left. The next day I nursed the champagne, but no one came. I was about to leave when a young man walked up to me.

"Are you Zia?" he asked.

I nodded.

"My name is Luigi. I am a friend of Jacqueline's. She can't see you." But he handed me an envelope.

"I'll be here tomorrow . . ." I started to say, but he was already on his way out. Who was he? Who was *she*? The whole thing was like a mystery. The envelope contained one of those cards you buy in a shop — sweet words, but the message was clear: "Good-bye." That only made things worse. I couldn't get her out of my mind; she was becoming an obsession.

I was there the next day, sure that I would never see her again.

I was wrong. She was waiting . . .

. . . with Luigi!

But she had literally come to say good-bye — she was going away.

"Will you see me when you return?"

"Maybe."

But maybe wasn't nearly enough. I told her that the matter was no longer in our hands — destiny had taken over. How else could she explain the way we had met? I also complained about the impersonal printed cards, and said
that I would have written something original.

"You're a gambler. Write something yourself and if I like it, I'll have dinner with you when I come back."

Infatuation inspired eloquence and I wrote:

I thought I saw a friendly wave,
But when I looked again, it was a wand that
waved its magic on my mind.
I sat to look into the coolness of your eyes
but saw instead the softness of your soul.
I tried to touch your hand, but it was gone,
already reaching out to steal my heart.
And when you walked away, you didn't leave
but stayed — a gentle whisper in my thoughts.

But would she like it?
She liked it.
We had dinner; this time she left Luigi behind.
And my losing streak?
What losing streak?

13

"Is it Losing?"

Miami, September 1986

The President of Pakistan, Mohammed Zia ul Haq, was speaking to me: "I wish you and your team the best of luck. Pakistan expects great things from you."

When the President of your country speaks, you listen Still, as he spoke, I was wondering if he realized that he had just confiscated half my house.

I was in the strangest position. On the one hand, it was because of the President, a great sports enthusiast, that bridge in Pakistan had finally been given official sanction — a huge step forward for our little band. Since Rye we had been allowed to compete regularly in international events, something almost unheard of a few years ago. On occasion, the players even had government help with expenses.

On the other hand, his government had just ordered the confiscation of half my house — my brother's half to be exact. With the advent of martial law under Zia ul Haq, my brother had once more found himself in the opposition. And again, he soon had charges made against him for anti-government activities, and this time, rather than spend another period in jail, he had taken political asylum in England. As a result, his property had been ordered to be confiscated: his half of the house we had jointly owned in Karachi. How you confiscate half a house is as unclear to you and me as it was to the bureaucracy. Fortunately at the time, thanks to the help of a bridge-loving policeman, and in spite of occasional visits by the local constabulary to inspect the inventory, the puzzle was still unsolved and the order had been restricted to a paper one. Perhaps if we did well in Miami, I could ask the President for a favor.

As usual, we weren't well prepared. For the 1986 Olympiad, countries were permitted to enter several teams. Two of our best players, Masood and Munir, were unable to participate. And our bridge association, in its wisdom, despite my vehement opposition, had seen fit to enter several teams-of-four into the Rosenblum (the Open Team Championship) rather than a fewer number of teams containing six players each.

The association wanted to give our players as much experience as possible. But this was naive. In as gruelling an event as the Rosenblum, you need six players on a team so that everyone has the chance to rest.

On the encouraging side, our women bridge players were happy. This was the first time they had been allowed to take part — a surprising development considering the strict codes in Muslim countries regarding women.

Our four-man team consisted of Nisar (Chance) and Nishat, in one room, while Fazli and I, playing together for the first time, were in the other. You will remember that we were all members of the original squad in Rye five years earlier.

The Rosenblum is essentially a knockout event and we were knocked out immediately. *Arrivedérci* — well, almost. The format of the tournament did allow one slight chance for a comeback — a one-in-a-thousand shot. Defeated teams were dumped together in the Swiss teams, where over 100 teams traded punches for four days until one team emerged to re-enter the Rosenblum semifinal. With bridge powers like America, Poland, France and Sweden each represented by several strong teams, all playing in the Swiss, we didn't have much hope — or did we?

Somehow the magic of Rye repeated itself. Once again our team started to dance through the opposition, team after team, match after match. We were nearly always completely outclassed, but something — maybe the goddess of Bridge — was constantly by our side. We just couldn't lose. I've never experienced anything like it.

If we needed something unexpected to happen, inevitably, it did. At times, good opponents would go crazy, having ridiculous misunderstandings against us. Once, on a recount, we squeaked through by one imp. If we bid a slam needing three finesses, a break and favorable lead, we would always get it — and we could almost claim before the opening lead. That's the way it was.

When the smoke cleared at the end of the four days of almost non-stop play from 10 in the morning to two or three the next morning, we somehow emerged, bruised and battered, at the top of the pack, eligible to play in the semifinals.

Who says lightning doesn't strike twice? To be fair, our team members had played above ourselves — "out of their skins" — but we had needed much more than that, and we had found it. Now there were four teams left, three from the United States and us.

Our players are colorful characters. Add the fact that we were "no-hopers" — the only obstacle standing in the way of mighty America — and you'll understand why all the non-Americans, and even many Americans, were behind us. Players from every corner of the globe came up and wished us luck. The Canadians, long-time friends of ours, handed out T-shirts with the words "Paki-Power" printed on them. Everyone wanted to show their support.

We would need it.

Our opponents in the semifinal were the odds-on favorites to win the event. A crack team bristling with talent: Ronnie Rubin, Mike Becker, Peter Weichsel, Michael Lawrence, and our tormentors from Rye, Jeff Meckstroth and Eric Rodwell — or *Meckwell*, as they are now known.

From the first board, the 64-board match turned out to be a tug of war. The lead swung back and forth. With 16 boards (one session) to go, the score stood at America 127, Pakistan 105.

Things had been going the Americans' way. Now with only a few boards left, I could feel there was nothing in it.

Fazli and I sat against Meckstroth and Rodwell in the Open Room on VuGraph. In an auditorium, a large audience would be able to follow the play as it was televised from the playing room. Commentators would keep the audience informed and amused during those periods when the players were thinking.

It all came down to the last three hands — the most exciting I've ever played. We didn't know it at the time, but at this point we were 11 imps behind the U.S. Play in the Closed Room, where Nisar and Nishat had faced Lawrence and Weichsel, was over and the players had rushed to the VuGraph to watch the finish. A commentator asked Weichsel how his results had been. He replied confidently that the Americans had had the best of all three hands; he felt they couldn't lose. The audience, mostly Pakistani supporters, was quiet, sad that our gallant try was about to fail.

"Board 59," the commentator called.

[The Open Room, where we were seated, had started with the last three boards, numbers 62, 63 and 64. Therefore, we were playing numbers 59, 60 and 61 last. This allowed a comparison of results with the Closed Room, where the hands had been played in the normal sequence, so that the running score was known by the audience.]

The hands presented here, starting on the next page, have been rotated to make South the declarer (for the reader's convenience):

North dealer
None vulnerable

```
                        North
                        ♠ A 10 3 2
                        ♡ —
                        ◇ K Q 8 5
                        ♣ J 10 7 3 2
West                                         East
♠ 9                                          ♠ Q 8 6 5 4
♡ Q 8 6 5 3         ┌─────────┐              ♡ A 7 2
◇ A 7 3            │         │              ◇ 9 4 2
♣ A Q 9 4          │         │              ♣ 8 6
                    └─────────┘
                        South
                        ♠ K J 7
                        ♡ K J 10 9 4
                        ◇ J 10 6
                        ♣ K 5
```

Open Room:

Fazli	Meckstroth	Zia	Rodwell
West	North	East	South
—	1 ◇*	pass	1 ♡
pass	1 ♠	pass	2 ♣*
pass	3 ♡*	pass	3 NT
(all pass)			

1 ◇ = Precision
2 ♣ = fourth suit forcing
3 ♡ = a splinter bid in hearts!

Closed Room:

Weichsel	Nisar	Lawrence	Nishat
West	North	East	South
—	1 ♣	pass	1 ♡
pass	1 ♠	pass	2 ◊*
pass	3 ◊	pass	3 NT
(all pass)			

2 ◊ = fourth suit forcing

The hand was displayed on the screen, with the bidding from the Closed Room. Our teammates had bid to the aggressive three-notrump contract.

The defense had been quick and deadly. Weichsel (West) had found the precise sequence of plays necessary to defeat the contract. He led the ♡5, Lawrence winning with the ace and returning the suit to the jack and queen. Now Weichsel switched to the ♣4. Nishat won in the dummy with the 10 and led a diamond to the jack, which Weichsel ducked. Nishat led another diamond. Weichsel went in with the ace, and cashed his two club tricks to defeat the game. Nice play.

In our room, Meckstroth and Rodwell were in the same contract. If the Americans made three notrump, their lead would be overwhelming. Weichsel had read the cards brilliantly — could we do the same?

Fazli also led the ♡5, and on my heart return won with his queen. He hardly stopped for breath — he also led back the ♣4! Plus 50 for East-West. Fazli had found the same defense as Weichsel, almost card for card. (Fazli didn't duck the ◊A for one round.) Cheers shook the building; we were still in the game.

Board 60 came next:

East dealer
North-South vulnerable

```
                      North
                      ♠ 10 8 4 3
                      ♡ A 8 7 5
                      ◇ J 10 8
                      ♣ A 2
West                                  East
♠ K                                   ♠ A 7
♡ Q J 9          ┌─────┐              ♡ 10 6 4 2
◇ A Q 6 5        │     │              ◇ 9 4 3
♣ J 9 8 6 5      └─────┘              ♣ K 7 4 3
                      South
                      ♠ Q J 9 6 5 2
                      ♡ K 3
                      ◇ K 7 2
                      ♣ Q 10
```

Closed Room:

Weichsel	Nisar	Lawrence	Nishat
West	North	East	South
—	—	pass	2 ◇*
pass	3 ◇*	pass	3 ♠
(all pass)			

2 ◇ = the Multi: either a weak two-bid in a major or
     a strong two-bid in a minor
3 ◇ = "Please bid your major at the three-level"

Our Closed Room result of three spades one down, minus
100, was normal. Again it didn't look hopeful. If Meckstroth
and Rodwell could stop in two spades, they would pick up
points; and if they got to three spades, there would be no
swing.

Open Room:

Fazli	Meckstroth	Zia	Rodwell
West	North	East	South
—	—	pass	1 ♠
double	4 ♠	double	(all pass)

However *Meckwell* like to bid a lot. Rodwell's one-spade opening was light, but because they play Precision, it was limited to 15 high-card points.

Fazli's double was a little light, too, because he didn't have four hearts.

Meckstroth jumped to four spades — the lightest action of all, but, as usual, he was applying the maximum pressure. However, preempting in spades usually leaves the opponents with no option but to double. They are unlikely to bid at the five-level when they have had no chance to exchange information about suits.

I did double; and for once I was at least closer to having my values than the rest of the table.

The audience roared with delight. The play was identical in both rooms. Both Wests led the ♡Q, declarer winning with the king. A heart to the ace, a heart ruff, and the ♠Q followed. The Wests won with the ♠K and switched to a low club. Declarer had to lose one club, two diamonds and two spade tricks. Four spades was two down, giving Pakistan 9 imps.

With one board to go, we were behind by 2 imps.

The audience was on the edge of its seats, enthralled. Meanwhile, on the screen, the last hand appeared:

North dealer
All vulnerable

                    North
                    ♠ K J 2
                    ♡ Q 10
                    ◊ A 9 6 2
                    ♣ A 6 3 2

West   East
♠ 7   ♠ 9 8 5 4
♡ A K 8 7 5 3   ♡ J
◊ K 10 5   ◊ Q 8 4 3
♣ Q 9 5   ♣ J 10 7 4

                    South
                    ♠ A Q 10 6 3
                    ♡ 9 6 4 2
                    ◊ J 7
                    ♣ K 8

Closed Room:

Lawrence	Nishat	Weichsel	Nisar
West	North	East	South
—	1 NT*	pass	2 ♣*
2 ♡	pass	pass	2 ♠
(all pass)			

1 NT = 12-14 points
2 ♣ = non-forcing Stayman

It looked like it was all over. Nishat and Nisar had, for once, been conservative, stopping in two spades making four: +170.

The commentators announced that four spades was unbeatable. If *Meckwell* bid four spades, they would pick up some more points; and if they stayed out of game, we would *push* the board. Either way, we would lose the match.

The bidding was super-scientific:

Open Room:

Zia	Rodwell	Fazli	Meckstroth
West	North	East	South
—	1 ◇	pass	2 ♠*
pass	4 ♠	(all pass)	

2 ♠ = a game-try with five spades and four hearts

Warned that the heart lead might not be best, I led the ♣5 to the 2, 10 and king. Meckstroth played a club to the ace, ruffed a club in hand, and exited with a low heart, which I won with the king.

Suddenly, one of the commentators, Michael Rosenberg, noticed something. It was possible, just possible, that four spades could be defeated. There was one line of defense, improbable but possible, that would defeat this contract — if only we could find it. Try to spot the killing defense. This was the position with West to play:

North
♠ K J 2
♡ Q
♢ A 9 6 2
♣ 6

West (Zia)
♠ 7
♡ A 8 7 5 3
♢ K 10 5
♣ —

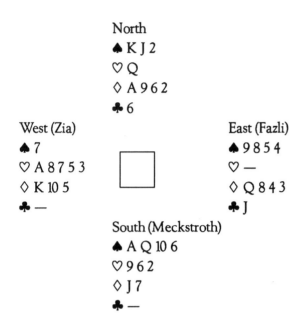

East (Fazli)
♠ 9 8 5 4
♡ —
♢ Q 8 4 3
♣ J

South (Meckstroth)
♠ A Q 10 6
♡ 9 6 2
♢ J 7
♣ —

The winning defense required that I play a trump at this point. When Meckstroth won in the dummy and played a second heart, Fazli had to ruff, even though he would be ruffing a trick I could win with the ace, to play a second trump. Nothing else would succeed.

The audience shouted me on, willing me to play a trump. (Being quite a way from the auditorium, we couldn't hear.) But after a long time-out for thought, I found the trump switch, and the audience cheered so loudly that we *could* actually hear the roar in the room. Meckstroth looked up at me; we both knew the hand must be critical.

It wasn't over. Meckstroth called for the ♡Q. The spotlight was now on Fazli. Would he ruff? This was real theater.

Once again, he was up to it. He ruffed my trick, and played back a spade! One down, +100, and 7 imps to Pakistan. We had beaten one of the finest teams in the world by 5 imps.

The hotel erupted. Friends, supporters, anyone, everyone, rushed out to congratulate us.

Suddenly a voice called out, "Pakistan zindabad!" Another followed.

The cry was taken up. The sound echoed throughout the hotel as everyone chanted, "Long live Pakistan!" It was a proud moment.

Unfortunately, there was little time for celebration. The match finished at three in the morning, and the final would start at ten the next morning. Not nearly enough time to get the rest we badly needed.

On the way up to our rooms, I congratulated Fazli on his play throughout the day, especially over the last three hands. "You did brilliantly to ruff the heart on the last hand when you knew I had the ace."

His reply left me stunned: "How do I know you had the ace, you fool! You didn't lead a heart from ace-king. I ruffed the trick because I thought Meckstroth had the ace!"

It's five years later, and I'm still not sure whether he was serious or not.

The final was an anti-climax. We had done as much as we were able, and once more our miraculous luck deserted us at the last moment. It was almost as if someone were saying to us, "I'd like to encourage you, but it really would be too much for you to win." Here is an example:

North dealer
All vulnerable

                        North
                        ♠ 8 7
                        ♡ 9 7
                        ◊ A 10 9 8 2
                        ♣ 9 6 5 3

West   East
♠ A Q 10 6 5   ♠ J 9 4 2
♡ J 8   ♡ A K 6 5 4
◊ —   ◊ K 6 5
♣ K Q J 10 7 4   ♣ A

                        South
                        ♠ K 3
                        ♡ Q 10 3 2
                        ◊ Q J 7 4 3
                        ♣ 8 2

Open Room:

Nishat	Silverman	Nisar	Lipsitz
West	North	East	South
—	2 ◊	double	pass
3 ◊	pass	3 ♡	pass
3 ♠	pass	4 ♣	pass
4 ◊	pass	4 ♠	pass
4 NT	pass	5 ♡	pass
6 ♣	pass	7 ♣	pass
pass	double	7 ◊	pass
7 ♡	double	(all pass)	

Closed Room:

Woolsey	Fazli	Manfield	Zia
West	North	East	South
—	pass	2 ◊	pass
4 ◊	double	4 NT	pass
6 ♠	(all pass)		

In our room (Closed Room), Ed Manfield's two-diamond opening was Flannery, which showed a minimum opening with four spades and five hearts. Kit Woolsey's four-diamond response announced, in principle, slam interest in spades and a singleton heart! Manfield used Roman Keycard Black-wood, and Woolsey jumped to try to describe his void. They had an "accident" but landed on their feet, winning all 13 tricks for +1460.

In the Open Room, Neil Silverman had been studying SAPP. His two-diamond opening showed a weak two-bid in hearts, diamonds or clubs, or a weak minor two-suiter, or some strong possibilities. After that a confused auction ensued. Seven clubs would have made, of course, but Silverman found a well-timed double, thinking his ◊ A was cashing. Nisar had been trying to get to the right major-suit game, so he tried once more with seven diamonds.

By this time Nishat thought the whole thing had been a bad dream — he bid seven hearts, one grand slam they couldn't make.

Seven hearts doubled went two down for minus 500 and 18 imps to the U.S.A. If Nishat had bid seven spades, Silverman would have doubled, but it would have been laydown. We would have gained 14 imps: a swing of 32 imps!

At the time, people suggested that our poor play in the final was due to our exhaustion. I hope I refuted that in the daily bulletin, where I wrote an article in which I mentioned that our opponents had completely outplayed us and thoroughly deserved their win. And I added from my heart:

"*Is it really losing when hundreds of people from far-flung corners emotionally will you to win as if you were their own team? We became not just a Pakistan team, but the representative of the rest of the world. Was that losing?*"

14

Inside Out and Upside Down

Miami, September 1986 — More Great Hands

Although not as dramatic as the ending of the semifinal
match described in the previous chapter, there were other
very exciting hands in Miami.

The following one, also from the semifinal, must be a
candidate for the most amusing hand ever played in a world
championship. On the score-card it appeared as one solitary
imp to Pakistan, but the actual story is much more complex.

This was the hand:

West dealer
North-South vulnerable

```
                        North
                        ♠ K 3 2
                        ♡ Q 5
                        ◊ K 10 8 5 4 2
                        ♣ 7 6
West                                        East
♠ J 10 8 7 5                                ♠ A Q 9
♡ 9 4 3 2                    ┌─────┐        ♡ 8 6
◊ Q                         │     │        ◊ A J 7
♣ J 10 9                    └─────┘        ♣ A K Q 5 4
                        South
                        ♠ 6 4
                        ♡ A K J 10 7
                        ◊ 9 6 3
                        ♣ 8 3 2
```

Open Room:

Rubin	Nisar	Becker	Nishat
West	North	East	South
1 ♠ ! (1)	1 NT (2)	double (3)	pass (4)
2 ♣ (5)	pass (6)	pass (7)	2 NT (8)
pass	3 ◊ (9)	pass (10)	3 ♡ (11)
pass	pass	pass (12)	

(1) The perfect conditions for a psychic one spade.
(2) Either 16-18 balanced or a random hand, but only
     Chance would bid it at unfavorable vulnerability.
(3) When was the last time your partner opened the
     bidding, RHO bid one notrump vulnerable and
     you had 20 points?
(4) Nishat lets his partner do his thing.

(5) Rubin admits to his psyche.

(6) Nisar passes — to the relief of the Pakistani supporters.

(7) Knowing that partner has psyched, and worried about his club length, Becker passes. I wish my partners would give me dummies like this.

(8) Not sure what is happening, Nishat keeps the ball rolling.

(9) Nisar is an expert at running — so he runs.

(10) Becker decides that if his opponents have got this far, they must know what they're doing. If only he knew!

(11) Still not sure what Chance is doing, Nishat goes with his 100 honors.

(12) Happy that they didn't get to game!

Nishat was able to win five trump tricks. Pakistan: -400.

In the Closed Room, sanity prevailed:

Fazli	Weichsel	Zia	Lawrence
West	North	East	South
pass	pass	2 NT*	pass
3 ♣	pass	3 ◊	pass
3 ♠	pass	4 ♠	(all pass)

2 NT = 20-21 points

Fazli received a diamond lead. He won in the dummy and, to keep control, made the fine play of leading the ♠Q. In this way he retained control, driving out the ♠K while dummy could ruff the third round of hearts. We were +420, for a gain of one point for the Pakistan team.

They Bid My Suits First

If I told you I picked up a 6-5 distribution, first heard my partner overcall in my six-card suit and then the opponents bid and raise my five-card suit, you might say I was hallucinating. But it was true.

Bridge can be a funny game. Here is the hand:

North dealer
None vulnerable

```
                         North
                         ♠ K 9 7 2
                         ♡ 10
                         ♢ J 5
                         ♣ A K J 9 5 2
West (Zia)                                 East (Fazli)
♠ A J 10 5 4             ┌────────┐        ♠ —
♡ A K 9 6 4 2           │        │        ♡ Q J 7 5 3
♢ 10                    │        │        ♢ A 6 4 2
♣ 7                     └────────┘        ♣ 8 6 4 3
                         South
                         ♠ Q 8 6 3
                         ♡ 8
                         ♢ K Q 9 8 7 3
                         ♣ Q 10
```

Zia		*Fazli*	
West	North	East	South
—	1 ♣	1 ♡	1 ♠
pass	2 ♠	pass	3 ♢
pass	4 ♡	pass	4 ♠
4 NT	pass	5 ♢	double
6 ♡	pass	pass	7 ♢ !
double	(all pass)		

230

Fazli's overcall was light, but you must get into the auction with a distributional hand like that.

Before passing, I checked that both one spade and three diamonds were forcing. Four hearts was a splinter bid, which didn't surprise me.

I knew partner had at most one spade, and had the advantage that in our system four notrump was always Blackwood. But I was unlucky. South believed my questions and my bidding. I guess I tipped my hand.

We'll draw a veil across our defense. Suffice to say that we got only 300 after I made a stupid club lead.

Almost more amusing than the hand was the fact that the International Bridge Press Association judges conferred on me the Romex Award for my excellent bidding! This was a little ironic as the Romex Award is given by George Rosenkranz, and it was his Mexican team that had beaten us in the first round of the Rosenblum. Naturally I accepted the prize gratefully, but because it's now too late to give it back, I can confess that I wasn't being brilliant in the slightest. I was just thoroughly enjoying myself.

The Nine of Diamonds

Playing in the semifinals of the Olympiad Open Pairs, we approached a table where two rather serious Continental types were speaking to a lone kibitzer. This was the first hand:

South dealer
All vulnerable

North (Fazli)
♠ A Q 4
♡ Q 9 6 5 3
♢ Q 8 4 2
♣ A

☐

South (Zia)
♠ K J 2
♡ K 2
♢ A K 10 6
♣ K Q 3 2

Zia		Fazli	
South	West	North	East
1 ♢	pass	1 ♡	pass
2 NT	pass	3 ♢	pass
3 ♠	pass	4 ♣	pass
4 NT	pass	5 ♡	pass
6 ♢	(all pass)		

We bid briskly to six diamonds, and West led the ♣4. If the diamonds broke, the hand would be easy. I won the ♣A in dummy and led the ♢2 (9, K, 5).

Typical! The ♢9 forced me to think about a 4-1 diamond break. If West had four diamonds, I would need a friendly lie of the cards. If the diamonds were indeed 4-1, it would be much easier to handle if East were being tricky and had false-carded with ♢J-9-7-3. Then I could simply ruff a club and pick up the trumps.

It was clear that the answer lay in deciding just how good the East player was. Would he play the 9 from ♢J-9-7-3? How could I determine that? Perhaps I'd get a clue from his convention card. If these guys played something really complicated, I could mark them as experts. No, there were no giveaways. Their names seemed Swedish, so I tried a different approach. "Do you know P. O. Sundelin?"

No reply. Undeterred, I continued, "What do you think of upside-down signals?"

He ignored me.

I almost gave him a bidding problem, but rejected the idea. Finally, I gave up and decided that if I've never heard of him, he was more likely to be playing an honest card than a devious one. After all, he wasn't Garozzo.

I decided to trust his ◇9 and play for a miracle lie.

Wrong. When I cashed the ◇A, West discarded.

East *had* falsecarded — the simple line would have been successful.

This was the full deal:

North
♠ A Q 4
♡ Q 9 6 5 3
◇ Q 8 4 2
♣ A

West
♠ 9 7 5 3
♡ 10 7 4
◇ 5
♣ J 9 7 5 4

East
♠ 10 8 6
♡ A J 8
◇ J 9 7 3
♣ 10 8 6

South (Zia)
♠ K J 2
♡ K 2
◇ A K 10 6
♣ K Q 3 2

I left the table, furious with myself. But it was only as I

233

walked away that I suddenly realized why I should have known that he must have been a very good player, quite up to an expert falsecard. What had I overlooked?

The kibitzer! He had a kibitzer. In a select field where superstars abound and permission to watch is limited, the spectator had chosen to watch him rather than some of the greatest players in the world. He had to be top class.

I missed that — did you?

* * * * * * * * *

Returning home after Miami was a new experience. For the first time we were welcomed back, and the government even thought our efforts worthy of recognition, presenting us with medals for achievement in Pakistan bridge. We had come a long way.

15

Would You Like to Go to an Orgy?

The North American Nationals

There are three North American Bridge Championships, commonly known as the Nationals, every year. Each one is an orgy — of bridge. A long way from the classical music of European bridge events, this is Rock 'n' Roll, American style. I'll agree that the dress is pretty scruffy: the more fashionable ones wear jeans and a T-shirt. I'll agree that the schedule is anti-social: You play eight to ten hours of bridge a day, and eating hours are unnatural. I'll even agree that the conversation is limited: "Why did you lead a spade?" "How could you play a heart?"

But you'll have to admit that the level of competition is the highest in the world, and the atmosphere and experience irresistible. And all are welcome: novices, seniors, even insomniacs are sure to find a suitable game. And if you think you can handle it, you can match wits against the best.

Bridge is the only sport where a beginner can play against an expert. Could you imagine entering a golf tournament with Nick Faldo or Jack Nicklaus? Or playing a set of tennis against Ivan Lendl or John McEnroe? And for an entrance fee of only $20-$30 per day? There are no money prizes. The reward is pure — the pleasure of playing. Well, almost. If you're lucky or good enough to win, collecting one of the major national team titles also qualifies your team for the playoffs to select the United States national team. The trials winners usually end up as world champions. Just how long does it take to become a World Champion? Would you believe only one year? Impossible, you think?

It happened to Seymon Deutsch.

Seymon Deutsch is your everyday guy — your everyday Texas billionaire guy, that is, together with cowboy boots and private jet. (Don't fly in it — his ex-fighter pilots think they're still in Vietnam.) His college bridge games were long behind him; then, in August, 1987, he was sitting in his office in Laredo when a man entered unannounced. The stranger mentioned the word "insurance." Seymon promptly threw him out.

Not long after, Deutsch's telephone rang: "Why did you throw my partner out of your office?" Even after 20 years, the voice of Bobby Wolff was unmistakable. The insurance man had been *the* Bob Hamman — the top-ranked bridge player in the world over the last 20 years, and Wolff's bridge partner.

The incident revived Wolff's friendship with Deutsch, and also Deutsch's interest in bridge. They formed a team of Deutsch, Hamman, Wolff and Jim Jacoby.

The rest is history. They won the Grand National Teams. They added Jeff Meckstroth and Eric Rodwell, and won the U.S. Trials. In October 1988 in Venice, Italy, they beat Austria in the final to win the World Team Olympiad for the first time for the United States.

Not all the entrants in a Nationals, which range between five and ten thousand, depending upon the season of the year, can win a national team title. Most have to learn to live with losing all the time. But some find it harder to accept than others. Take the *Head-Banger*.

The Head-Banger is a well-known bridge player who *really hates* losing. In fact, a bad result blows a fuse. He starts banging his head against the nearest hard object, usually a wall. I'm not sure how that helps him, but he doesn't seem to stop. And to date no one's ever heard him complain of a headache.

Bridge players have no sympathy for such antics, as shown on the occasion when the H-B was pitted against a pair of degenerate gamblers who had made him the subject of a large bet. Ron, gambler number one, had bet Steve, gambler number two, that he could entice the H-B to go into his act during their forthcoming seven-board Swiss team match.

The bet didn't last long. This was what the H-B, sitting East, could see of the first board:

North
♠ 3 2
♡ A 9 8 4
◊ K Q 10 6 2
♣ 5 4

East (H-B)
♠ Q J 4
♡ K 3
◊ J 5 4 3
♣ J 10 6 2

Ron, South, was in six hearts. West, the H-B's partner, led the ♠7 (2, J, K). Declarer then finessed the ♡Q, losing to H-B's ♡K. Back came a low spade, which declarer *ruffed*.

Convinced that his partner had underled the ♠A at trick one and had handed his opponent a slam, the H-B couldn't stand it and started to bang his head against the table.

Gambler number one promptly stood up and whistled to gambler number two, pointing out that the H-B was banging his head. Steve saw this and reluctantly sent his losses across to Ron via one of the caddies. Once the money arrived, Ron sat down and said, "Oh, you led a spade. I'm sorry, I've revoked." He promptly replaced his trump, the revoke not having been established, with the ♠A.

The Great Equalizer

The 1988 Fall Nationals held at Anaheim, California, was the scene of one of my favorite wins. It was the prestigious Reisinger, and I was part of a team that wouldn't exist in any game except bridge.

Our strange collection consisted of: a Canadian Jew, an American Black Christian, an Indian Hindu and a Pakistan Muslim.*

Where else but bridge?

When someone asked me how we won (as usual, we weren't expected to), I replied, "With all the Gods rooting for us, how could we lose?"

I feel there is a key here. I'm sure that bridge can show the rest of the world how easy it is to live together, regardless of race, color, creed or social background. The only thing that interests a bridge player is his opponents' bidding and defensive carding methods. He doesn't care a hoot about anything else.

America's Best

The Lion of American bridge is undoubtedly Bob Hamman. No mention of the American bridge scene would be complete without one of his hands. The occasion was the 1985 U.S. Trials. The match was neck and neck when Hamman, sitting East, picked up this hand:

---

* Billy Cohen, Ron Smith, Jaggy Shivdasani and Zia

♠ A J 9 5 4 3 ♡ A K 5 ◊ 10 9 2 ♣ 2

With both sides vulnerable, he took part in this auction:

Bergen	Wolff	Cohen	Hamman
South	West	North	East
1 ♣	pass	1 ♡	2 ♠
3 ◊	4 ♠	pass	pass
4 NT*	pass	5 ◊	double
(all pass)			

4 NT = minor-suit take-out

His partner led the ♠7, and this was what he could see:

North
♠ Q 6 2
♡ 10 9 8 7 4 2
◊ J 8 5
♣ 7

East (Hamman)
♠ A J 9 5 4 3
♡ A K 5
◊ 10 9 2
♣ 2

Dummy played low, Hamman put in the ♠J, and declarer ruffed. Marty Bergen (South) cashed the ♣A (8, 7, 2). Next came the ♣3 (♣10, ◊5 . . .). Plan your defense.

This was the full deal:

239

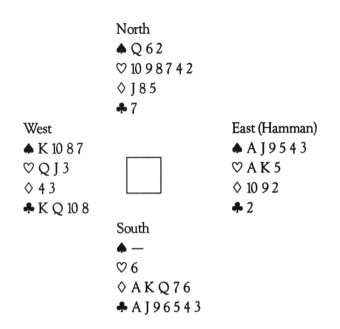

North
♠ Q 6 2
♡ 10 9 8 7 4 2
◇ J 8 5
♣ 7

West
♠ K 10 8 7
♡ Q J 3
◇ 4 3
♣ K Q 10 8

East (Hamman)
♠ A J 9 5 4 3
♡ A K 5
◇ 10 9 2
♣ 2

South
♠ —
♡ 6
◇ A K Q 7 6
♣ A J 9 6 5 4 3

Hamman made one of the best defensive plays ever. He didn't overruff. His play was so brilliant, I'm not even embarrassed to admit I wouldn't have even thought of it. Like most people, I would have automatically overruffed and played back a trump. On that defense, declarer would be only one down. But after Hamman's play, the declarer, who had to ruff himself down to return to his hand, lost control and finished three down: a penalty of 800.

In the other room the contract was also five diamonds doubled. However, there West led a trump, which resulted in two down. Hamman's team, therefore, gained 7 imps on the board, whereas if he had overruffed, they would have lost 7. The final margin in the match: 5 imps!

The Characters

The Nationals are full of weird and wonderful characters, and I've partnered most of them. G— is one of those players who hates to admit to a mistake. Once when I was playing with him, he overbid and went for a large number (1100). I had never opened my mouth in the auction and was wondering how he would try to squirm out this time. I found out! G— grabbed his opponents' cards and started screaming, "How could you double? You had nothing."

About to play a session with E—, I accidentally brushed against him. There was a hard object near his breast pocket. It wasn't a gun that I suspected, but a carrot on which he nibbled between hands. Bugs Bunny, beware.

X— never washes. He smells terrible; so bad in fact that his opponents are always in a hurry to get away from the table, with the consequence that they don't spend enough time working out their problems, thereby giving X— great results. Who can blame them?

I once approached a table where L—, a black (and overtly gay), was snapping his fingers in time to the tune coming over his walkman. I led a fancy ♠Q from ♠Q-10-3, which led to a disaster. The suit was divided like this:

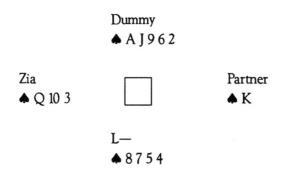

Naturally, I found the only card to give away the contract. Putting down his radio, L— chortled. "Don't you know never to lead a black queen against a black queen?"

It takes all sorts.

* * * * * * * *

The Nationals, together with the New York merry-go-round, were incentive enough for me to spend much more time in America. I took an apartment in the suitably named Trump Tower, and since then, whenever I can get over the jet lag and the occasional losing streak, I've been leading a very happy, if dissolute, life.

And then — there was Atlantic City.

New York is only a few hours' drive from the lights and tournament of Atlantic City. . . .

16

The Man

Atlantic City — Final Day

As we sat down for the final session, I thought of something Somerset Maugham once wrote: "Bridge is the most intelligent and diverting game that the wit of man has ever devised — I would have children taught it as a matter of course. You can play bridge as long as you can sit up at the table and tell one card from another. In fact, when all else fails, bridge remains."

Yes, but winning would make it that little bit sweeter. To the rest, this was the last day — the end of the tournament. To me it was the beginning. The lessons of Rye and Miami were still fresh in my mind. I knew how easy it was to have nothing left at this stage — and knew I had to avoid that trap.

As the Tournament Director called for silence, I went through my private check list:

1. Wake up.
2. Force my mind into a state of total alertness — aware

of every out-of-tempo breath around the table; every change of mood; every kind of feeling.

3. Focus on the ever-changing people around me; who are they? (What do I know about them? Do we speak the same bridge language? How do I get my partner to play his best?)

4. Think about the correct way to bid each hand, then go back and recheck. Make sure my reasoning was objective and my analysis not seduced by some flaw in my character.

5. Don't be lazy (my biggest problem); work hard at even the most simple-looking hands. Appearances can be deceiving. Initial reactions are frequently accurate, but there's no harm in confirming that these impressions are correct.

6. Try not to let anything interfere with my mind's ability to work its maximum. This is the most difficult. It is so easy to be distracted, so human to react emotionally to a disagreeable partner or opponent, or to a disaster, or even to a spectator sitting too close.

7. Most of all, think only about winning — nothing less would do.

If I did this on every hand, I would still need to play well and be in luck to beat some of the best minds in the game. Winning at bridge isn't easy, but that's the challenge.

I was tense and ready for action, but, frustratingly, I had to wait until halfway through the session before I had an opportunity to practice what I preach. Sitting East, I picked up:

♠ 7 ♡ Q 7 3 2 ◇ Q 7 6 2 ♣ A J 5 3

West	North	Zia East	South
—	—	pass	1 NT
pass	2 ♣	pass	2 ♠
pass	3 ♠	pass	4 ♠
pass	pass	?	

Hands with 4-4-4-1 shape are dangerous — with all the suits breaking badly, it's usually right to defend. This deal started off unremarkably, but things improved. My rubber-bridge years stood me in good stead.

Everything was ideal. The auction was limited. Trumps were breaking badly, and I needed to get moving. Besides, how many chances would I get?

"Double!"

I struck gold. This was the full deal:

North
♠ 8 5 4 3
♡ K 10 8 5 4
◊ A 4 3
♣ 2

West (Coon)
♠ A J 9 6
♡ J 9
◊ 10 9
♣ Q 9 8 7 4

East (Zia)
♠ 7
♡ Q 7 3 2
◊ Q 7 6 2
♣ A J 5 3

South
♠ K Q 10 2
♡ A 6
◊ K J 8 5
♣ K 10 6

The cards lay perfectly — for us. My partner, Charlie Coon, led a club to my ace. I returned a diamond, the jack being finessed successfully. Declarer entered dummy with a heart to the king, then led a trump up, playing his king. Coon ducked smoothly. Encouraged, declarer cashed the ♣K and ruffed a club. Hopeful, he led another trump. But when I showed out, he wished he hadn't. Coon took two trump tricks, then played clubs. Two down, +300 for East-West. It was a good pick-up.

Not long after, two of the leaders came to my table. This was a crucial round. The result would be doubly important because they were partnered against me. South was Peter Pender, at one time a figure-skating champion and subsequently a three-time world bridge champion. North was P. O. Sundelin, my old friend from the *Canberra* TV series. Yesterday he had been sharing the lead with me. Probably there was still nothing between us. My partner was a young woman whom I recognized but didn't know by name.

I needed a break, something to put a little distance between these two and me. I could never have imagined what followed.

North (Sundelin)
♠ A K 5 4
♡ 8 4 3 2
◇ K Q 4
♣ 9 5

West
♠ J 7 2
♡ Q 6
◇ 10 7 6 5
♣ J 8 4 3

East (Zia)
♠ 9 8
♡ K 9 7 5
◇ A 3 2
♣ A Q 10 2

South (Pender)
♠ Q 10 6 3
♡ A J 10
◇ J 9 8
♣ K 7 6

	Sundelin	Zia	Pender
West	North	East	South
—	—	1 ♣	pass
pass	double	pass	2 ♣
double	pass	pass	2 ♠
pass	3 ♠	pass	4 ♠
(all pass)			

North-South did well in the bidding. The game was good but close; there would be plenty of pairs stopping short. It looked bad for us.

North (Sundelin)
♠ A K 5 4
♡ 8 4 3 2
◊ K Q 4
♣ 9 5

West
♠ J 7 2
♡ Q 6
◊ 10 7 6 5
♣ J 8 4 3

East (Zia)
♠ 9 8
♡ K 9 7 5
◊ A 3 2
♣ A Q 10 2

South (Pender)
♠ Q 10 6 3
♡ A J 10
◊ J 9 8
♣ K 7 6

Two ladies came to my aid. The first lady was my partner — she doubled two clubs. On the low club lead, Pender played the ♣5 from dummy. Knowing from her double that she had either the king or jack of clubs, I played the ♣Q to keep communications open with my partner.

The second lady was Lady Luck.

Pender, sure that I was about to put up the ace of clubs, played the wrong card — the ♣6 instead of the king. When he saw the ♣Q and ♣6 sitting on the table, too late he realized his mistake. I won the trick with the queen, and we took another club trick, a diamond and a heart. Pender was down one in his cold contract.

The combination of circumstances was incredible. My closest rival, Sundelin, just *happened* to be his partner. My partner just *happened* to double two clubs (not an obvious action). I just *happened* to play the ♣Q. Pender's concentration just *happened* to slip for that one second.

Sundelin had watched in horror as his chances of winning disappeared when the ♣6 hit the table. As he left the table he graciously said, "Forget it, Peter. It could happen to anybody."

It was likely that this hand had ruined Sundelin's chances, but there were plenty of others in the race. My results continued to be mediocre. Anyone with a big session could overtake me. I needed to do something. I needed to *win*, as opposed to *not losing*. But time was running out. By now the pit was surrounded by a large crowd of silent faces. The atmosphere was electric. Sometimes I get a "feeling" — I got one on this last hand. Perhaps it was because Benito Garozzo — the champion of champions — was my opponent, or that another friend, Pamela Granovetter, was my partner; or perhaps it was just because the vibes were there. I don't know.

North (Pamela)
♠ A K 6 4 3
♡ J 8 4
◇ A Q J
♣ A 5

☐

South (Zia)
♠ Q 9
♡ K 6 5
◇ 10 9 7 5 4
♣ Q J 10

Garozzo	Pamela		Zia
West	North	East	South
pass	1 ♠	pass	1 NT
pass	3 NT	(all pass)	

Garozzo led the ♡10. I called for dummy's 4. East flinched slightly before playing the 3, and I won with the king. East's flinch told me the hearts were 4-3.

I counted my tricks: three spades (at least), one heart, one club (at least) and four diamonds after giving one up to the king — there was that king of diamonds again. It looked ridiculously easy.

Then why didn't it "feel" easy?

Could anything go wrong?

I went into the "tank" — isolating myself from everything around me to focus completely on the problem. If ever I needed to be in Heat #1!

It seemed natural to play a diamond to the jack. If that lost, I had nine tricks. What if the finesse won? I could either come back to hand with the ♠Q to finesse again, or play the ◊A-Q from the dummy (just in case East was ducking). I always had the spade break to fall back on, yet I was missing something. I made myself work harder. What if the diamonds didn't break? What if spades didn't break? *What if both suits didn't break?*

If I finessed successfully in diamonds, and continued with the ◊A-Q, Garozzo would duck his king if he had started with four. Then I would go down if spades weren't 3-3. There had to be an answer. Suddenly I saw it. The perfect play.

I finessed the ◊J — it won. Then I continued with the *queen* of diamonds *without* cashing the ace. If it lost, I had nine tricks. If it won and diamonds were 4-1, I could play on spades, giving up a spade trick if necessary.

It looked odd, even unnatural — it might even cost an overtrick or two. But it *felt* beautiful, it *was* beautiful, it was the reason I played bridge.

Ninety-nine times out of 100 it wouldn't make the slightest difference. Today it was the winning play. Garozzo won the diamond and switched to a club. I won the ace and made my contract. This was the full hand:

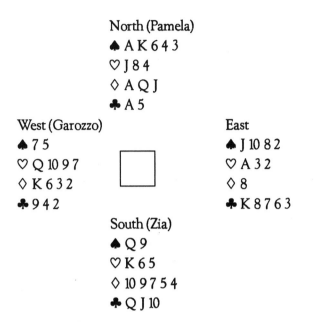

North (Pamela)
♠ A K 6 4 3
♡ J 8 4
◊ A Q J
♣ A 5

West (Garozzo)
♠ 7 5
♡ Q 10 9 7
◊ K 6 3 2
♣ 9 4 2

East
♠ J 10 8 2
♡ A 3 2
◊ 8
♣ K 8 7 6 3

South (Zia)
♠ Q 9
♡ K 6 5
◊ 10 9 7 5 4
♣ Q J 10

The audience was still thinking about my unusual play, but my partner, Pamela, who is co-editor of *Bridge Today* magazine and always looking for a column hand, knew it was special. She was hurriedly writing down the hand, but paused to comment, "Nice play, Zee — I bet you win the whole thing."

She was right. At that moment I knew I had won.

I was The Man.

The results confirmed it:

Position	Country	Score (imps)
1) Zia	Pakistan	96
2) Fred Hamilton	USA	79
3) P. O. Sundelin	Sweden	77

At the prize-winning banquet, even the Weasel confirmed

it. Discussing the last hand, he told me, "Now that's *one* contract my daughter would not have made." I couldn't have been paid a greater compliment.

Omar presented the prizes. The casino had a man with a briefcase (just like in the movies) filled with new $100 bills. The winners — maybe they'd lose some of it back in the casino — could cash their checks if they preferred. They preferred!

Tim Holland congratulated me, insisting on buying the champagne. He smiled and said, "I can afford it. I won more from Louie than you won in the tournament." He had played backgammon nonstop for two days.

It transpired that Louie had been losing so much that he suggested increasing the stakes for the last game from the last four digits on the bank note to the last *five* digits. Tim agreed and won. As they checked the note, the two left-hand digits were 9 and 8. "Keep the change!" said Tim.

We decided to drive back that night, but not before I went to the casino for one last time.

"Don't lose all of your money," someone shouted.

The casino was almost empty.

"Hey, Zia! What happened to my camels?" For a change, Sarah Jane was at the roulette table. I joined her. The maximum bet on a number was $200. So I gave her $200 and asked for a chip.

"One chip?"

"Yes." I placed it on number one. I stood to win $7,000. The ball spun dizzily inside the wheel, then slowing, caressed the "1", before it fell close beside it. "Thirteen black — you lose." She sounded sad. I smiled.

You can't lose when you've already won. As I walked away, I heard someone ask her, "Who is that guy? Is he some kind of big-time gambler?"

And her reply:

"No — just a bridge player."

Bridge Books by Natco Press

To Bid or Not to Bid (The Law of Total Tricks)
    by Larry Cohen   ..... $12.95 ea.

Following the Law
    by Larry Cohen   ..... $12.95 ea.

Bridge My Way
    by Zia Mahmood   ..... $12.95 ea.

Also Available

Better Bidding with Bergen (Vol. I)
   Uncontested Auctions
    by Marty Bergen   ..... $10.95 ea.

Better Bidding with Bergen (Vol. II)
   Contested Auctions
    by Marty Bergen   ..... $10.95 ea.

To order any of these books please send check or money order (please **add $3.00 postage/handling**) to:

Larry Cohen
181 Longhill Rd. I-6
Little Falls, NJ 07424